College Bound for Christians

A Christian Living Adulting Guide to Help Navigate Mental Health, Your Purpose, Friendship, College, Dating, and Faith

Peter Christian

© *Copyright 2024 Peter Christian - All rights reserved.*

The contents of this book may not be reproduced, duplicated, or transmitted without direct written permission from the author.

Under no circumstances will any legal responsibility or blame be held against the publisher for any reparation, damages, or monetary loss due to the information herein, either directly or indirectly.

Legal Notice:
This book is copyright-protected. This is only for personal use. You cannot amend, distribute, sell, use, quote, or paraphrase any part or the content within this book without the consent of the author.

Disclaimer Notice:
Please note the information contained within this document is for educational and entertainment purposes only. The website addresses recommended throughout this book are offered as a resource. They are not intended in any way to be or imply an endorsement, nor is the content contained there on vouched for. Every attempt has been made to provide accurate, up-to-date, and reliable complete information. No warranties of any kind are expressed or implied. Readers acknowledge that the author is not engaging in the rendering of legal, financial, medical, or professional advice. The content of this book has been derived from various sources. Please consult a licensed professional before attempting any techniques outlined in this book.

By reading this document, the reader agrees that under no circumstances is the author responsible for any losses, direct or indirect, which are incurred as a result of the use of the information contained within this document, including, but not limited to, —errors, omissions, or inaccuracies.

I wish to dedicate this book to my loving wife and family who have encouraged me to write and to God who has shown me Grace every day.

Thank you!

Thank you for choosing my book! As a token of gratitude, I'm thrilled to offer you a FREE companion journal to download.

To receive your free journal, please email support@lapublishings.com with the subject, Christian Living Journal.

Or click here: https://lapublishings.aweb.page/p/a7e17635-be2a-486f-88f2-2c4ae99cb100

This journal is your space to reflect on your faith journey, with meaningful prayer and gratitude tracking pages, and to collect your college experiences. Also pages with this book's prayers and scriptures.

Thats not all! I want to give you the opportunity to have access to my upcoming books when on promotion, and valuable emails that I am excited to share with you. I will not be emailing everyday it will be along the lines of devotionals and self-help thoughts.

Scan the QR code for emails and journal.

Table of Contents

INTRODUCTION	1
What to Expect When You're Graduating	1
What's Next?	3
Responsibly Independent	5
Crossing the Threshold	7
Chapter 1 Tips and Tricks for College	9
#1: Form Good Dining Hall Habits	9
#2: Get to Know Campus Before Classes Start	11
#3: Put Yourself Out There	11
#4: Take Advantage of Office Hours	11
#5: Research Potential Career Fields	12
#6: Organize your Schedule	13
#7: Avoid Buying Books at the Campus Bookstore (If You Can)	15
#8: Don't Stress Too Much About Your Grades	16
#9: Read Professor Reviews Before Choosing Your Classes	16
#10: If You Aren't Certain About Your Major, Take Your Gen-Eds First	17
#11: Call Your Parents	18
#12: Pack an Umbrella	19
#13: Work With Your Academic Advisor	19
#14: If You Can Avoid It, Don't Room with a Good Friend	20
#15: Get Flip Flops for the Communal Showers.	22
Other Useful Tools and Resources	22
20 College Must-Haves	26
Chapter 2 Work… Meaning Homework	31
#1: Take Your Classes Seriously (It's the Godly Thing to Do)	32
#2: Learn How to Take Notes	39

#3: Learn How to Study — 46

#4: Learn How to Fight Procrastination — 50

Chapter 3 Finding a New Church — **56**

What Church Is — 57

What Church Is Not — 58

How to Find a Church — 59

Chapter 4 Finding New Friends — **65**

What Does the Bible Say About Friendship? — 66

6 Traits to Look for in a Godly Friend — 67

Where to Meet Godly Friends — 74

Chapter 5 Dating — **78**

Deciding Your Deal-Breakers — 79

4 Things to Look For in a Godly Partner — 90

Chapter 6 Mental Health — **97**

Keeping Tabs on Your Mental Health — 99

#1: Stress — 99

#2: Anxiety — 102

#3 Depression — 105

#4 Self-Esteem — 109

Chapter 7 Finding Your Purpose — **115**

What is My Second Purpose? — 116

#1: Know Your Spiritual Gifts — 117

#2 Find Your Passion — 120

#3 Ask a Mentor — 124

#4 Pray About It — 127

Chapter 8 Keeping the Faith — **129**

How to Keep the Faith — 131

To Wrap it up. — 135

Thank you and what's coming! — **138**

References — **139**

About Peter Christian — **144**

INTRODUCTION

What to Expect When You're Graduating

"And the one sitting on the throne said, "Look, I am making everything new!" And then he said to me, "Write this down, for what I tell you is trustworthy and true."

- Revelation 21:5

So, you're about to graduate high school. Congratulations! That was a crazy four years, right?

Right now, you must be reflecting on all the memories. Hopefully, the good ones outweigh the bad. Those Friday night lights, halftime band performances, the school play, after school and weekends with your friends, class trips, prom and homecoming, maybe a few well-deserved after-school detentions (don't worry, I won't tell). All of these things and more come together to form the quintessential high school experience.

Did you enjoy your high school experience? What did you get out of it? Maybe you learned a few things from your stack of textbooks—a little bit of math, English, or a foreign language sprinkled in here and there? Did you learn to lift weights for the first time in gym class or during off-season prep for your sport of choice? Did you learn how to bake in Home-Ec or how to change your car's oil in shop class? Hopefully, you stored away a few of these life lessons that helped turn you into the more mature person you are today. But none of that answers my first question: Did you enjoy high school?

You might have heard a few teachers tell you that "these are the best days of your life." You'll hear it in dramatic teenage TV shows from time to time as well. It's a common phrase with a misunderstood point, and you secretly hope it's not true. There's just no way those four short years of high school are as good as it gets.

Well, let me calm your nerves. It's not! High school is neither the best nor most fulfilling years of your life. On its face, this age-old sentiment seems silly. In my opinion, it also comes across as sad. *"The best days of my life? Maybe for you, but not for me."*

What they're trying to convey, even if poorly delivered, is that you should enjoy high school! You should soak up the moments and take advantage of this phase in your life when responsibilities are few and possibilities are many. In a roundabout way, they're communicating their own regrets. Like me, they tried to get through high school as fast as possible so they could graduate to adulthood. They didn't soak up the moments or take advantage of life without bills, children, and bosses.

Don't judge your teachers as I did. They miss their youth and wish like crazy they could get it back. They ache for the days when their number one concern was getting their college applications submitted on time. You'll have to take my word for it for now, but life's demands only increase as you get older. Your teachers envy where you are in life, and they want to impart their wisdom so you don't make the same mistakes as they did.

I'll ask my question a final time: Did you enjoy high school?

If your answer is no, and the last four years seem like an inconsequential blur, don't sweat it. Pack it away as a lesson learned. Use it to guide how you live your next phase of life, because life doesn't end here. You have a lot to look forward to!

What's Next?

Your next era of life comes with many perks and privileges. Soon, you'll have your own place. Near the top of your college to-do list is "move into the dorm room." While moving is rarely fun, setting up your space–your solace, your own little corner of the university–is a blast! Do you catch yourself daydreaming about your first apartment or dorm? Do you imagine decorating, cafeteria dinner, dorm parties, being just steps away from your friends, and FINALLY being out of your parent's house? The first step into your dorm or apartment signifies massive change, from which you'll likely never turn back.

Soon, you'll begin your new job: *learning*. Your task over the next four years is to internalize the knowledge for your chosen field and to check the necessary boxes for entering the workforce. Now, some classes are more useful than others, and some aren't at all applicable to the field you hope to enter. Some of the electives on your course schedule probably seem like a waste of time, but every grade matters. Therefore, every class matters, regardless of the subject.

Everyone around you will be a stranger. You'll likely have no friends and be all alone. Forgive me for sounding so dark and sad, but it's true. The only thing you'll know about the unfamiliar souls with whom you share the sidewalks and hallways will be what they look like. They'll appear more confident and sure of themselves than you'll feel, but believe me, they're wearing the same shoes as you: the *"faking-it-till-I-make-it"* shoes. Nearly every fellow student you cross paths with is still figuring it out. That's the beauty of college; You get to figure it out together.

You don't have to be alone because everyone else is in the same boat, and it's a crowded boat. Is it true that you can be alone in a crowd? Yes. It's up to you to ensure you're not a lonely, bored passenger on a cruise ship full of party people.

College is a great place to make life-long friends, and every stranger you come in contact with is a potential friend. Many fall in love in college, while others defer dating until after their time on campus has expired. There's nothing wrong with either road. Perhaps the best part of college is that the people you meet all seem to have crossed some magical "maturity bridge."

You might be surprised to learn that much of the petty nonsense that ruled the halls of high school is nowhere to be found on a college campus. People are generally treated with more respect in college. No one has the time to be a mean girl, bully you, or think about the embarrassing thing you did in second period. Everyone has their own lives, and they're now mature enough to know theirs is none of your business, and yours is none of theirs. *Thank the Lord*, right? *Good riddance, silly drama!*

Responsibly Independent

College is an incredibly unique experience every graduate talks about for the rest of their life. You will never forget it. Ask your parents, an older sibling, or any other adult, and they'll tell you all about their college experience. They'll have vivid memories, and they'll speak of them with a smile on their face.

Part of this unique experience is produced by the campus lifestyle. This lifestyle shares a few things in common with the "real world" inhabited by wage-earning, bill-paying, child-raising adults such as your parents. But at the same time, it's wholly different.

Imagine the real world and college form a Venn diagram. Within the overlap, you'll find things such as money. Both life in the real world and life in college are exorbitantly expensive. Ask anyone in their thirties, and they'll tell you, *"I spend $100 before I even wake up."* And we've all heard about the high, and still rising, cost of earning a degree.

More importantly, you'll find words like "independence." Both worlds have a lot of that. Your first taste of true independence comes during college. You get to wake up when you want, eat when you want, choose your own class times, exercise when you want, go to bed when you want, and sleep as much as you want. Your schedule is 100% yours, as opposed to living at home when your time is 100% your parents'!

The most important word at the intersection of the real world and college, in my opinion, is "responsibility." It's the common denominator shared by the world your parents inhabit and college.

Life is now a yin and yang. With independence comes responsibility. They're two sides of the same coin. Now that it's up to you when, how, and if you do anything, all of the consequences are yours as well. If you choose to be undisciplined with your diet, you'll suffer the consequences of the dreaded "freshman fifteen." If you choose to be undisciplined with your studies, you'll suffer the consequences of being put on probation.

Leaving home means you get to become your own person. You can shed any and all of your family's expectations. They're not around to enforce them, so what do you care? You can now live life how you see fit. You get a chance to make it your own. This can either be extremely liberating or terrifying.

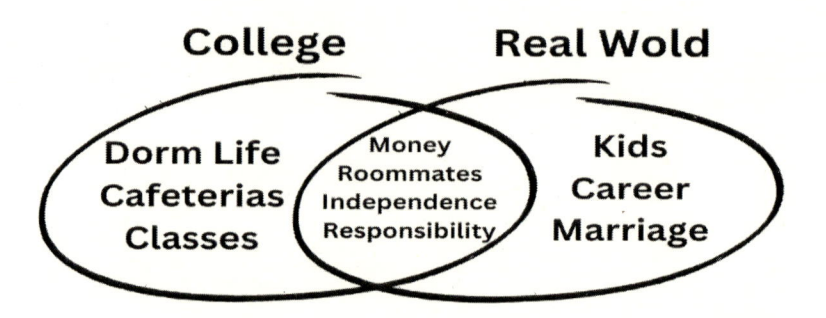

College / **Real Wold**

- Dorm Life
- Cafeterias
- Classes

(Overlap: Money, Roommates, Independence, Responsibility)

- Kids
- Career
- Marriage

Crossing the Threshold

My next question (perhaps you're asking it as well) is: with all this new and exciting change, does anything stay the same? With all that's on the horizon, what about the things that are now behind you?

I hope there's one thing you carry into this next phase of life: your FAITH.

As children, grade schoolers, and high schoolers, our parents' faith is often our faith. What they believe, we believe. You go to church because they go to church. You go to summer camp and school-year youth group nights because, well, Mom and Dad said so. But guess what… That's all over. Now, it's up to you whether you practice your faith. It's up to you to decide for yourself whether you believe any of this stuff in the first place.

If you do want to keep your faith throughout college and onward, then this book is here to help.

This book aims to help you reconcile your faith with college life. How do you do both at the same time? How do you take on college in a Christ-like way? How do you do adult things in a way that makes Him greater?

In the following chapters, we'll go over:

- Tips and tricks for surviving in college
- How to succeed in your classes from a Christian perspective
- How to find a new church
- How to find Christian friends
- How to find a Christian significant other
- How to care for your mental health
- How to find your purpose
- How to keep the faith

Read it and take it seriously, and I think this book could make you more than capable of tackling all the independence and responsibility you have headed your way and coming out a better Christian on the other side.

Chapter 1

Tips and Tricks for College

"Intelligent people are always ready to learn. Their ears are open for knowledge."
- Proverbs 18:15

Before we get into the serious advice about Christian college life, let's cover some basic tips and tricks for school. There are more YouTube videos by current college students with advice for incoming freshmen than could ever be counted. Some have great advice. Others should probably just be deleted. I've watched more than I care to admit and have read through several blogs and Reddit threads on the same topic.

Take this advice to heart. It comes from people who were in your shoes just a few short years ago. It's wise to learn from the failures and successes of others and to avoid reinventing the wheel. Here are the 15 best tips I've found on the internet:

#1: Form Good Dining Hall Habits

Recent studies show that a healthy diet is good for your brain. According to Ohio State University, a diet limited in refined sugars and saturated fats and rich in healthy fats, fruits, vegetables, whole grains, and legumes can improve brain function and help prevent cognitive decline. Who knew brain power was a side effect of broccoli?

Dining halls offer a huge variety of buffet-style food, and most of it is super unhealthy. All the pizza, burgers, ice cream, and other S-tier stuff you could ever eat will be at your fingertips for every meal. Be sure and resist the urge to only eat junk food and fight off the dreaded freshman fifteen.

How to Form Good Dining Hall Habits:

- **Survey what's available**. Your campus could have multiple dining halls, and the best one might not be the one closest to you. Once you pick your preferred hall, look over the options. Don't just dive right in as soon as you walk through the door. Look at what each station has to offer and decide what you'll eat before you pick up a plate.

- **Prioritize fruits and veggies**. Whether raw or cooked, it's a good strategy to fill half your plate with veggies and fruit before choosing anything else. This leaves less room for the junk you're craving.

- **Take small snack breaks**. Snacking throughout the day is good for 2 reasons:

    1. A small calorie boost will keep you energized and focused during classes and in between mealtimes.
    2. It'll help keep you from gorging in the dining hall.

But of course, they should be healthy snacks! Eating fewer meals during the day is a perfect recipe for accidentally eating bigger meals when you do eat. Being too hungry when you eat almost always leads to overeating.

#2: Get to Know Campus Before Classes Start

You might want to move in a few weeks early to learn your class schedule and find the buildings and classrooms where they'll take place. College campuses can be huge, and the buildings can look like Hogwarts-esque mazes. You don't want to risk any tardies by searching for your classrooms on the first day.

#3: Put Yourself Out There

Don't be afraid to join clubs, fraternities, or intramural sports teams. Seek out social scenarios that will provide opportunities to meet people and make friends.

Extracurriculars also look great on a resume. They show potential employers you can maintain a work-life balance with minimal people skills.

#4: Take Advantage of Office Hours

Almost every class you take in college will have office hours. Office hours are times you can meet with the professor or teaching assistant (TA) outside of class. Sometimes, a professor and TA will each have their own office hours to take advantage of.

Office hours are great for asking questions about assignments or concepts you've covered in class. Many professors will tell you there's a direct correlation between people who go to office hours and people who do well in their classes. Your odds of receiving some leniency increase if the grader has an emotional connection to you. In other words, it's harder for the professor to fail you if you're a good student.

#5: Research Potential Career Fields

Think you know what you want to be when you grow up? Just wait a year. That life-long career dream might not look so sweet after taking a few courses. I used to think I wanted to be a civil engineer before realizing the math it required.

Jokes aside, choosing a career path is a tough and important choice. It's a bit unfair society has saddled teenagers and young adults with such a weighty decision. It isn't something to be taken lightly.

It's not like you have one opportunity to choose and that's it forever—you're stuck. Thankfully, it doesn't work that way. You're always welcome to change your major if you want.

However, it's better if you change your mind sooner rather than later. If you switch it up your senior year, you might just be forced to have a super-senior semester or two to meet the course requirements or pack your schedule so full of classes that you can hardly breathe. No one wants that.

So what can you do? You can do some research. Here are a few ideas:

- Talk to an upperclassman, professor, or teaching assistant who's in the career field you're interested in. They'll be able to tell you what things are like behind the curtain.

- Take major-required courses freshman year to see if you even like the course material. If the course material is boring, I wouldn't expect work out in the real world to be any better.

By course material, I don't mean the homework, group projects, or assigned reading. That stuff is always boring! But if the concepts covered in the class don't catch your eye, you might consider a different major.

- Take a career aptitude test. This can help you better identify your interests and skill sets. This one from the Princeton Review is pretty good:

https://www.princetonreview.com/quiz/career-quiz

#6: Organize your Schedule

Keeping a well-organized schedule can help ensure you remain productive. More importantly, it can be the make-or-break factor when it comes to meeting all your deadlines. It's unbelievably easy to lose track of assignments, notes, and due dates when you're taking 4 to 5 classes simultaneously.

Here are a few strategies for organizing your schedule:

- **Organize everything by class.** Have a single notebook and folder for every class for any hand-held materials that are passed out. If you're taking notes with a computer, then this is too easy. Just make a folder for each class and organize accordingly.

- **Start using Google or Apple Calendar.** This is probably the easiest way to track due dates. A physical calendar or a planner are valid options until you make a mistake and need to erase everything you just wrote.

- **Make a to-do list.** Organize everything you have due from soonest to latest, with soonest at the top. That's what you're working on next. You can also organize your to-dos using a priority quadrant like this:

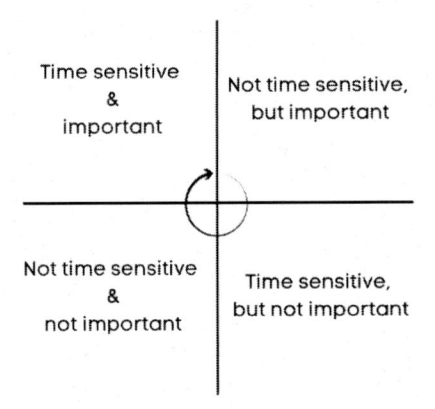

Time sensitive & important	Not time sensitive, but important
Not time sensitive & not important	Time sensitive, but not important

Plot all of your tasks and assignments according to which quadrant describes them best. Then, starting in the top left, work your way through them clockwise around the quadrant.

- **Plan your week ahead**. Sitting down on a Sunday and memorizing what's due in each class for the upcoming week is a great strategy for staying organized. This isn't as ambitious as it sounds because many classes you take will have a regular assignment schedule. Homework will usually be due on the same day at the same time. If you have any exams outside of midterms and finals, those will likely be on a regular schedule as well.

Another tip: If you can avoid it, don't schedule any classes on Friday. Having a 3-day weekend every weekend is so sick!

#7: Avoid Buying Books at the Campus Bookstore (If You Can)

Every university has a bookstore where you can buy basic school supplies as well as all the books your professors *will tell you* are required for their classes. The thing is, the bookstore is the most expensive place to get those things.

You should check out used retailers first. A few good ones are:

- Amazon
- Chegg.com
- Thriftbooks.com
- eCampus.com

Go to the class first to determine whether you need the book at all. If you must buy one, ask if an older, probably cheaper version will work for the class.

#8: Don't Stress Too Much About Your Grades

This sounds like crazy advice. Doesn't a good GPA determine everything about the rest of your life? Nope.

In truth, few employers care or ever ask for your GPA. Your first job out of college as an entry-level whatever? Yeah, they might ask you to list your GPA on your application, but they likely won't verify it or dig any deeper during an interview.

Internships are a different story. Your GPA really matters when it comes to getting a competitive internship. But here's the thing: getting a prestigious internship isn't anything to stress over, either. Employers won't care who your freshman year internship was with. As long as there's a name there, you'll get full credit.

The point is… It's important to get good grades, but don't sacrifice everything at the 4.0 altar. After all, grades don't define who you are. There is much more to life than your GPA, and I promise, in 10 years, you'll have a hard time even remembering what you graduated with.

#9: Read Professor Reviews Before Choosing Your Classes

The professor can make or break a class. A good professor can make the driest subjects interesting, but a bad professor can kill your dreams and make your semester miserable.

Luckily, you can essentially browse for your professors in college. Many big classes, like a popular gen-ed, are taught by multiple professors. Sometimes, a class like ECON 101 will have three different professors simultaneously teaching the class. As long as the seats are open, you can usually choose any of the three.

That means you need to research the good professors so you know which specific classes to pick. The best tool for this job is ratemyprofessors.com. This website has difficulty levels, quality scores, and written reviews from students for thousands and thousands of professors across the country. It can also tell you if you need a textbook for the class (but verify this because classes sometimes change their textbook requirements).

Do your research, and as long as you register for classes early enough, feel free to lock down all the easy and engaging professors.

#10: If You Aren't Certain About Your Major, Take Your Gen-Eds First

Your college class schedule will be very flexible. You can pretty much structure it however you want. That means you have all the freedom to take all your gen-eds right up front or save them for later for a nice and soft senior year.

If you've picked a major but are having second thoughts, or if you haven't picked a major but you're narrowing it down, take your gen-eds first. This will give you more time to consider your major before taking any upper-level classes. If you take major-required classes your freshman year but change your major later on, those major-related classes you took might not count toward your new major, making them a huge waste of time.

Taking a bunch of gen-eds up front is also a good way to explore your major! Schedule a variety of gen-eds across different fields and see what happens. Maybe something will spark your interest.

If you're 100% set on your major, you can take major classes now. This will mean you have gen-eds left for your junior and senior years, which will make those years much easier and more enjoyable.

#11: Call Your Parents

Your parents love you and are proud of you, and they know you're busy starting a life out on your own, but they'd sure love to hear from you once in a while.

I know it doesn't seem like it now, but you'll eventually realize that your parents really do have more life experience than you and have already answered many of the questions you're asking yourself now. Talk to them about these things. Pick their brain occasionally and allow them to do the same to you. Your relationship with your parents is turning a very important corner right now. Your parents are no longer your caretakers, disciplinarians, and sworn enemies. Now, they're potential friends.

Additionally, if your parents are paying for your college, don't you think the least you can do is check in with them a few times a week? Seems like a fair trade to me, but I'm pretty biased, considering I have kids of my own.

#12: Pack an Umbrella

For some reason, an umbrella just isn't something everyone thinks of when leaving for the day. No one thinks they'll get caught in the rain until they do. Do yourself a favor and go through the struggle of logging onto Amazon and buying an umbrella. You won't look like a grown, mature, responsible adult if you show up to class soaked to the bone.

#13: Work With Your Academic Advisor

So far, we've talked a lot about class schedules and how to get the most out of one. You might find yourself stressing a bit about setting your class schedule. Do you have questions like *"Why does picking classes seem like so much work? How do I know what classes I can and cannot take? How do I know what classes I need to take? How do I even actually schedule a class?"*

If this sounds like you, I have some news to help you relax: Meeting with your advisor can answer all those questions.

If you don't know what an advisor is, it's a university employee who guides you through your college career. All college students are assigned one at some point before their first semester and will usually work with the same one until they graduate. If you don't know who yours is, you should take a quick break from this book to look them up.

Advisors are by far your best tool for getting the most out of your class schedule. They have all sorts of other great advice and know what classes you need to take and how to sign up. Your advisor can sit down with you, take what major you'd like to graduate with, and create an entire freshman through senior year course schedule. It's like they're drawing you a map to the graduation stage.

Advisors can also help you change majors. If you ever decide to change your major, your advisor can tell you exactly what you need to do. They'll create a new course map like the one described above for your new major.

Advisors can also help you pick your major and what elective classes to take. They know what questions to ask to help you decide what you'd like to do for a living. Once they get to know you, they might even know better than you which major you'd enjoy. They also know which professors are good and how students usually perform in classes. If there's an easy class to take, they'll know what it is.

#14: If You Can Avoid It, Don't Room with a Good Friend

This advice has circulated for generations.

Honestly, the outcome of rooming with a friend just depends on how well you know your friend. Many discover while rooming with their friend how the person lives in their private life, and they don't like it. But some say they had no problems rooming with their bestie. Others even say it made their friendship stronger!

In general, the safe bet is choosing not to room with a friend for these reasons:

1. **Money can complicate relationships**. How awkward would it be for you to have to press your bestie for this month's rent? What if they just don't have the money? Are you willing to cover their share? Are you willing to have the management company kick them out? How would any friendship survive an eviction?

2. **Your friend might secretly be a slob**. They look and smell fine at school, and their locker isn't a disaster, but do you know what their room looks like? For all you know, it's full of old dishes, rotten food, dirty clothes, and a nasty shower. Trust me, if that's how their room looks now, that's how it will look in college.

What's the big deal? It's their room, right? Not my room, not my problem. Well, that's only true in an apartment. In a dorm, their mess is your mess. Also, their mess is guaranteed to spill into common space, whether it's a dorm or an apartment. They *will* leave dirty dishes, trash, laundry, books, papers, and shoes in the living room, dining room, and kitchen, and they'll leave hair in the drain and expired, moldy food in the fridge.

What if they're a neat freak? Could you handle getting a lecture every time you leave your backpack on the couch or one little grease splat in the microwave?

Their mess or even OCD will cause fights and strain your friendship. What happens when you can't put up with it anymore and are forced to part ways? How many friendships could survive one despising the lifestyle of the other?

3. **It will be harder to make new friends**. I can't lie; living with your best friend would be tons of fun at times. But this could mean you don't have any motivation to go and meet new people. Why meet new friends when you have such a fun time already with an old friend?

This is an unproductive mindset. One of the things at the top of your list to complete in college is to meet people. A large network of friends and fellow professionals is one of the greatest assets you can leave college with.

#15: Get Flip Flops for the Communal Showers.

Unless you want some gnarly athlete's feet, get shower shoes. Things are about to get real communal, real fast.

Other Useful Tools and Resources

1. **Grammarly.com**: Grammarly is a cloud-based writing tool that helps you write better. It offers feedback outside of grammar and spelling errors. For example, Grammarly can make suggestions to improve your delivery, make your writing more engaging, and improve clarity.

2. **Khanacademy.org**: Khan Academy is a free online learning platform. It has over 8,000 instructional videos on a wide variety of topics. Khan Academy is a great resource for times you need to hear something explained differently. Your professors won't always teach the same way that you learn. Khan Academy can help close the gap a little bit.

3. **ChatGPT**: While ChatGPT is a fascinating tool, you should exercise caution when using it. Sometimes, the algorithm "hallucinates" information. This is when incorrect or irrelevant information is mixed in with accurate and useful information. When using ChatGPT, be sure to double-check its output.

One great use, though, is creating citations. You'll be using a ton of citations in college! Every time you write a paper or essay and need to cite a source, just hop into ChatGPT and type in "Create a [Chicago, AP, etc.] style citation for this article: [insert link]." 85% of the time, it will generate a usable citation. Trust me when I say this will save you a ton of time.

4. **Campus writing centers**: Writing centers on your campus are there to help students become better writers. You can bring homework to them, and they'll coach you on a few ways it could be better.

5. **Campus tutoring centers**: Most colleges and universities offer some form of free tutoring for their students having a tough time with the course material. Your college could offer tutoring services in the

form of:
- One-on-one peer tutoring
- Weekly group study sessions
- Supplemental instruction for difficult classes
- Independent study
- Tutoring in small groups
- Virtual or in-person tutoring

6. **Campus resume services**: If you're an underclassman who's searching for an internship or applying for study abroad, or you're a senior who's begun the job hunt, you might need help crafting the best resume you can. College resume services can help you do that. They have resume professionals who have written hundreds of resumes and who know what employers are looking for.

7. **Campus career centers**: Career centers on your campus can help you prepare for a job hunt or help you during your job hunt. They also help with:
   - Job search skills
   - Identifying and working toward career goals
   - Finding suitable careers or graduate school programs
   - Getting referrals to employers
   - Boosting networking skills
   - Building professional skills
   - Preparing to enter the job market or graduate education
   - Choosing a major and minor based on career goals
   - Advising on when to take certain courses

- Working one-on-one with professionally trained career coaches
- Taking tests to identify skills and interests
- Finding career-related projects and academic experiences

8. **There are tons of software discounts available to college students, such as:**
    - Adobe Education
    - Autodesk
    - Atlassian
    - Axure
    - GitHub
    - Intel Free Software Tools
    - Microsoft Office for Students
    - MSC Software
    - On the Hub
    - Tableau

9. **Tons of tech companies have device discounts:**
    - Acer
    - Apple
    - Best Buy Student Deals
    - Dell
    - HP
    - Lenovo Student Discount Program
    - Logitech
    - Newegg Premier for Students
    - Microsoft

- Samsung
- Adorama
- DJI
- GoPro
- Skullcandy

10. **If you traveled far from home for college, you could probably use some discounted travel prices from companies such as:**
    - Amtrak
    - CheapTickets
    - CLEAR
    - Greyhound
    - Hotels.com
    - IKON Pass
    - Lonely Planet
    - Megabus
    - Sixt
    - StudentUniverse

20 College Must-Haves

1. **Shower caddy and hygiene bag.** No one likes awkwardly fumbling your soap, sponge, towel, toothbrush, and floss down the dorm hallway. Get yourself a hygiene bag and a shower caddy to make your trips to the dorm bathrooms less of a headache.

2. **Shower shoes.** You do not want to be the person that gets or gives

athletes foot. The floors of communal college showers are some of the nastiest surfaces on the planet. Don't put your bare skin against it. Use shower shoes.

3. **Mattress topper**. The mattresses furnished by your dorm or apartment will likely be old and uncomfortable. If you can't afford a new mattress, a mattress topper can be a cheaper solution to having a comfortable bed.

4. **Backpack**. For obvious reasons, you'll want a way to carry around your books, computer, and school supplies. Get a good backpack, and it can last you well beyond your college years.

5. **Laundry bag**. This is how you transport your laundry from your room to the laundry room. It also makes a nice dirty clothes receptacle so you don't have dirty clothes lying all over your room.

6. **Noise-canceling headphones**. These come in handy when people around you won't be quiet.

7. **Basic office supplies**. This includes:
    - Stapler and staples
    - Tape
    - Pens
    - Pencils
    - Scissors
    - Paper

- A printer (your library will have printers, but having your own really comes in handy)
- Note cards
- Sticky notes
- Notebooks
- A calendar planner
- USB flash drive
- Power strip
- Highlighters
- Binders
- Folders
- Book tabs
- Paper clips
- Command strips and hooks (These are useful for hanging things from walls or doors like towels, bookbags, hoodies, clothes, etc.)

8. **Storage bins/hanging closet**: These will help you organize your stuff and get the most out of your small college space.

9. **Extra sheets, pillowcases, and blankets:** Please don't go a month without washing your bedsheets. You should wash them at least every other week. More frequently would be even better. While your sheets are in the laundry, you'll need an extra pair of sheets to sleep on.

10. **Dishes/microwavable bowls:** If you're living in an unfurnished apartment, you'll need a full dish set, including pots, pans, baking sheets, silverware, blows, and plates. If you're living in a dorm,

disposable plates, bowls, and silverware might be a better option, but a few microwavable bowls will still come in handy.

11. **Coffee maker:** You'll want coffee on tap when it's time for final exams. Not having to go to Starbucks to get your caffeine fix will save you time and money. Unless you just dont drink coffee.

12. **Clothes hangers**: Your dorm or apartment won't come with any.

13. **Cordless vacuum**: That's right, no one's sweeping those floors but you.

14. **Basic household tools**:
- Duct tape
- Flat-head and Phillips-head screwdriver
- Flashlight
- Adjustable crescent wrench
- Hammer
- Jump start battery
- Tape measurer

15. **Portable phone charger:** Some days, you'll be out on campus all day going from class to class or activity to activity. You won't always have the option to sit in a seat with access to an outlet. So bring along a portable phone charger for those long days.

16. **Lap desk:** This is a small, angled table with cushions on the bottom.

Your laptop sits on top of the desk while the desk is in your lap. Lap desks make working while sitting on a couch or on a bed more ergonomic. The angle of the table supports your wrists, and the slightly elevated surface helps with downward neck tilt.

17. **Power strip:** This will make sure there are enough outlets for all your devices.

18. **Towels:** You'll need hand towels, hand cloths, and large towels for your dorm or apartment.

19. **Office chair**: If you plan on studying at home much, then it might be wise to invest in a comfortable and ergonomic chair. The right chair can increase your study stamina because you won't be worried about any joint or muscle pain.

20. **Mini freezer:** Mini freezers are a great spot to store study snacks and some refreshments.

Pray this Prayer

Lord, help me to learn from the experience of others. Let me see the wisdom in their actions and act wisely in my own life. Lower my pride so I'm not afraid to ask for help when needed. Lord, give me the courage to put myself out there and the discipline to keep myself organized. Bless me with an academic advisor who cares and can guide me in my search for a career.

Chapter 2

Work... Meaning Homework

"Work willingly at whatever you do, as though you were working for the Lord rather than for people. Remember that the Lord will give you an inheritance as your reward, and that the Master you are serving is Christ."

- Colossians 3:23-24

Chapter Two begins with serious advice on living as a Christian student. Starting now, I'll be giving you the needed advice and instructions to keep and practice your faith as a young adult.

Our first topic is work. You may or may not have to work a regular, hourly job during college. Many people are in a tight spot and need to work to afford books, tuition, and other expenses. Some people are lucky enough that their parents pay for their school. Still, others could be on a scholarship, getting money from the military, or several other scenarios.

While not everyone works a regular job in college, every college student has one form of work in common: homework.

Classes? Homework? Studying? Oh, right—the parts of college you've thought least about. You better start thinking about them now, because there's *plenty* of work waiting for you in college.

Which sparks a question: How do you do it right? How do you get the most out of class and your study sessions so you can crush your tests? Are there any tricks to note-taking and memorizing the course material?

You may or may not have had a class in high school that taught note-taking and studying techniques. If you didn't, I'm sorry your school failed you in this way. Don't you think it's something we should all be taught? How could they expect you to just show up to high school with skills you've never had a reason to use before?

If you did have a study skills class in high school, then this chapter might be a bit of a refresher, but still a worthwhile read. For those of you that are playing catch-up, focus in. The next chapter will prove useful throughout the next four years and beyond. You will carry these studying and note-taking skills with you not just into your senior year, but into your professional years as well.

#1: Take Your Classes Seriously (It's the Godly Thing to Do)

Before we get into study skills, let me say one thing: A common–but detrimental–belief about college is that the work will be just as hard as it was in high school. Beware this attitude. It's a "I didn't have to study in high school, so I won't have to study in college" mindset, and it's entirely wrong.

Look, I'm sure you're smart. After all, you got accepted into college! But homework, tests, and projects are not the same in college as they were in high school.

For one, college tests are way harder. Doing well on college midterms and finals requires critical thinking, not just rote memorization. Professors want to know that you actually understand the topic; they don't care what percentage of your notes you've managed to commit to memory. Expect more open-ended questions that will take you half a page to answer. You may have had classes like this in high school, and you should expect nearly every college class you take to be structured similarly.

If there's one thing to know about college classes, it's that some are intentionally developed for you to fail. I'm not kidding. Some classes are built to be so challenging almost no one can pass. Does that mean everyone gets an F come grade time? Of course not. Students often leave these classes with a good grade because of a grading curve.

A grading curve is a system that adjusts student grades so a test or assignment is properly distributed throughout the class. Professors, TAs, and other faculty members will sit down and decide what they want the average grade to be for a test. Come test time, they adjust the scores until the class's average meets their goal. These are always the really hard classes. Depending on how malevolent the department is, the target grade average is sometimes a crappy grade like a D. Technical subjects like math, physics, medicine, and chemistry always have notoriously hard tests like this.

Plus, tests will often have questions on topics never discussed in class! Sometimes, a test question will come from a footnote at the bottom of a page of the textbook. Professors and TAs can be sneaky like that.

Secondly, projects last longer in college. Some classes are fundamentally one big project. You'll work with your team during class time, and probably all get the same grade based on your collective work.

If a good GPA doesn't motivate you to take your classes seriously, then consider this: You should work hard at your classes and take them seriously because it's the Christian thing to do. The Bible is very clear regarding God's feelings about work:

"Pay careful attention to your own work, for then you will get the satisfaction of a job well done, and you won't need to compare yourself to anyone else. For we are each responsible for our own conduct."
- Galatians 6:4-5

"Lazy people want much but get little, but those who work hard will prosper."
- Proverbs 13:4

"Work brings profit, but mere talk leads to poverty!"
- Proverbs 13:23

"But those who won't care for their relatives, especially those in their own household, have denied the true faith. Such people are worse than unbelievers."
- 1 Timothy 5:8

These verses can be summarized in one sentence: We work hard to bless others and ourselves. If we make an honest effort at our work, it will eventually produce fruit we can feel proud of and use to provide for our family.

Can you see how your college work is no different? The effort you put in now will eventually impact you and your family. If you take college seriously, you'll leave with good grades, a good network, and plenty of career opportunities.

I want to be careful not to turn this into a prosperity message. This is a type of message taught in some churches that says God rewards faith with riches and good health. The Bible doesn't say God will make us rich if we have enough faith. In fact, the Bible doesn't really promise anything in this world other than pain and suffering in return for our faith. If your motivations for faithful work are fame, glory, and riches, then you've got it all twisted.

What I'm talking about is not the prosperity gospel. It's the idea we read about in Galatians 6:4-7. Because we have free will, we are responsible for our own conduct. This means we have to deal with the negative consequences of our actions, but it also means we receive the positive consequences of our actions. If you work hard in college, the consequence may be graduating with full employment already lined up. Good for you!

That being said, wealth is not inherently sinful. Yes, greed is bad, but greed is not synonymous with wealth. So, if you work hard and God makes you rich, count your blessings, maintain a pure heart, and use your wealth to bless your family and your neighbors.

As the scriptures remind us to stay humble and give all we have to follow Him:

"It is easier for a camel to go through the eye of a needle than for a rich man to enter the kingdom of God."

- Matthew 19:24

Most importantly, the Bible says we should work hard because it brings glory to God:

So, whether you eat or drink, or whatever you do, do everything for the glory of God.

- 1 Corinthians 10:31

God wants us to serve as Christ's example at all times and in all places. This means we should exhibit Christ-like qualities in the workplace and in school. We should have good attitudes, be polite, and in general, do more than is expected of us. What kind of impression would laziness, carelessness, and indifference toward the future give others about yourself and other Christians?

Think about the sermon on the mount. Jesus said, *"If a soldier demands that you carry his gear for a mile, carry it two miles."* This was in reference to an old Roman law that allowed Roman soldiers to grab anyone off the street and force them to carry their gear for 1,000 paces. The law was rightfully despised by the Jewish people and plenty of Gentiles, I'm sure.

Despite how humiliating the law may have been, what does Jesus say? What is the principle of the passage? It comes down to this: If someone curses you, bless them. If your boss asks you to stay late, respond in a kind and positive way. If your coworker takes credit for something you did, forgive them and move on. Don't go seeking revenge. Christians behave this way because Jesus wants us to love above and beyond what is reasonably expected of us.

Taking this Christian attitude towards work into college will pay out tenfold when it comes to your performance. Christians don't cut corners, lie, or shirk their duties at the expense of others. They don't procrastinate or make up excuses for failing to meet expectations. If you do things right, you'll learn more and learn better.

Don't just take my word for it! You'll be shocked when you see how many of your classmates just don't show up to class. Many come to lecture the first week to get the syllabus, then disappear. Compare how those people's class performance with your own. As long as you're not in a class full of geniuses, you'll see that you're a step ahead of your peers come grade time.

The same goes for taking advantage of extra credit. Can you believe some classes will offer enough extra credit that you can fail your final exam and still get an A in the class? There are many stories like this all over college Reddit threads. Good students take as much extra credit as they can get because it's the smart thing to do. If something is smart, why wouldn't you do it?

Having a good attitude toward class will endear you to your professors and TAs as well. Professors always light up when students have questions; it means that the student is taking an interest in the course (which also happens to double as their career). Professors always prefer attentive, involved students to lazy, distracted ones. How would you feel if someone was texting or scrolling TikTok while you delivered a lecture you prepped hours for?

In sum, we work hard because the Lord wants us to take advantage of what's been given to us. College education is a privilege—one that the vast majority of humans who have ever lived will never have. So don't take it for granted! Work diligently, and you'll be proud of what you accomplish.

Think about it in terms of the Parable of the Three Servants (Matthew 25:14-30). In this parable, Jesus tells the story of three servants. Their master gives them each a bag of money to take care of while he is away on business. One invests it and doubles the original amount. The second servant manages to earn 50% on the original amount. When he returns home, the master is very pleased with these two servants. But the third servant? He buried the money and earned nothing back. What happens to him? The master goes into a fury, calls him wicked and lazy, and throws the servant out into the darkness.

In the words of theologian William Barclay, this passage teaches that the only way to keep a gift is to use it. If God gives us something, we should use it to his glory. This includes the gift of intellect and the gift of a college education. Use it or lose it, folks.

That being said, working hard doesn't mean working dumb. We don't work for the sake of work; our work should be efficient and accomplish something.

What does working efficiently in college look like? In the pages between now and Chapter 3, we'll go over some studying, note-taking, and memorization tricks and tactics you can use to exceed in all your classes. Know them and use them, and you'll set yourself up for academic success.

#2: Learn How to Take Notes

Let's start with note-taking. Forget about taking notes on your laptop. You'll hate yourself for the moment, but thank yourself later.

Taking notes on your laptop is much easier than taking them by hand, and your laptop is built to organize all your work. Typing your notes seems like the obvious answer, as it's so much more efficient!

The problem is that there's a ton of research that shows you retain more information by writing something than you do by typing. According to an article published in *Psychological Science Magazine*, "students who took notes on laptops performed worse on conceptual questions than students who took notes longhand. We show that whereas taking more notes can be beneficial, laptop note takers' tendency to transcribe lectures verbatim rather than processing information and reframing it in their own words is detrimental to learning."

The article explains that students who take notes by hand have to process the information they're hearing and seeing. They can't write at the speed of spoken word, so they have to summarize it, rephrase it, and put it into their own words. Most people can type fast enough to record word for word what the professor says. This requires no information processing and thus makes the information less memorable.

In their report on the *Physiological Science* article, the BBC calls by-hand note-taking "note making." They say it's "an active involvement in making sense and meaning for later reflection, study or sharing of notes to compare understanding with lab partners or classmates." That's the British way of saying, *"You remember more if you take notes by hand."*

If I've convinced you to keep your laptop in your bag when it's note-taking time, then I suppose It's my responsibility to give you some advice as to *how* to take notes.

Effective Note-Taking

There are some common-sense things you can do to take effective notes. Taking good notes is important because good notes make for good test scores. Plus, isn't the name of the game in all of this efficiency? Don't you want to make sure you capture as much information as possible and commit as much of it to memory as you can on the first go around? If you do, then follow these seven tips:

1. When you're going over conceptual information during class, focus on the main points. Don't copy everything in the presentation word for

word. If you can't keep up and miss a few notes, you can always fill in the gaps after class.

2. Going back over your notes within 24 hours of class can help with retention, especially for factual information. When dealing with point-by-point, factual topics, writing everything down word for word can be beneficial.

3. Make a list of questions and thoughts you have during lectures that you want to follow up on later with a professor or TA.

4. Write down keywords, important dates, important names, or other information that stands out to you. Then, go back and define them later.

5. Make sure your notes look clean and the structure makes sense. Don't write notes on the same topic on different parts of the page.

6. Use abbreviations and symbols when you can. You should also write in bullets and phrases instead of complete sentences to save time and focus on the main concepts.

7. Use the same note-taking method for all your notes. Find a format that works for you and stick with it.

Speaking of note-taking methods… What are those?

A note-taking method is a way to organize the information you're recording. If the seven tips above are the tools for note-taking, then your note-taking method is the type of box you put your tools in.

Top 3 Note-Taking Methods

There are a ton of note-taking methods out there. We'll just go over the best 3.

1. The Cornell Method

The Cornell note-taking method was developed by Cornell University professor Walter Pauk in the 1950s. According to its advocates, it's perfect for summarizing notes and typically leads to better comprehension.

To use the Cornell Method, first divide your paper into three columns: in-class notes, cue column, and summary.

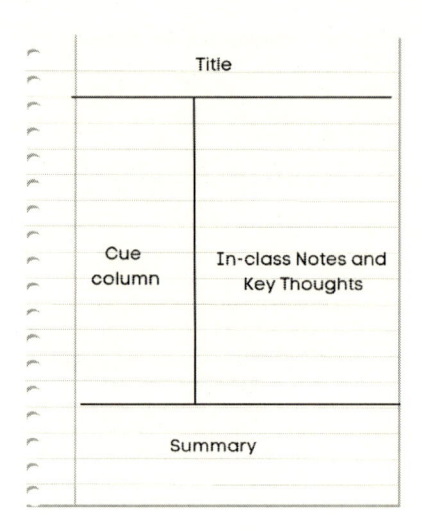

```
                    Title
         ┌─────────┬──────────────────┐
         │         │                  │
         │  Cue    │  In-class Notes and
         │ column  │   Key Thoughts
         │         │                  │
         │         │                  │
         ├─────────┴──────────────────┤
         │         Summary            │
         └────────────────────────────┘
```

The **in-class notes** section should be about 6 inches wide and 9 inches long. This is where you'll write short, concise class notes. Be sure to leave plenty of space between each note so you can go back and fill in more on each topic after class.

The **cue column** should take up the remaining width of the paper and should also be about 9 inches long. This is essentially the highlights column. Here, you'll write any questions you have during class or keywords you need to review later. Make sure each question or keyword aligns with any related notes in the in-class notes area. Review this column after class and answer the questions you wrote down, as well as define any keywords. You can use this section to quiz yourself throughout the semester, so you have less to study when it's exam crunch time.

The **Summary** section goes at the bottom of the page. It should be the entire width of the page and about 2 inches tall. This is where you summarize what you've written in both the in-class notes and cue column sections. When it comes time to study, you can quickly scan the summary section to see what relevant notes may be on that page.

2. Outline Method

The outline method is one of the most popular note-taking methods. It's a simple, linear way to organize class information according to major points and subpoints.

The outline method uses bullet points and indented sub-bullet points. Each indented sub-bullet should expand on the bullet point above it. This way, related information is closely grouped on the page. The outline method is best used in lectures utilizing presentation slides. When done correctly, the outline method makes it easy to review information according to each major topic.

To use the outline method, start at the top left of the page. Furthest to the left is where you'll put the main topics or ideas covered in class. As the professor presents the information and moves from slide to slide, you'll add more main topics. Below your main topic bullet points is where all the related information for that topic goes. Each time you want to add a sub-bullet point that expands on the bullet point above it, you should indent to the right, like this:

- Main topic
- Sub-topic
- Sub-point expanding on the subtopic
- Sub-sub-point that expands on the above subpoint

3. The Mapping Method

The mapping method is similar to the outline method in that it keeps related information grouped together on the page. It is a simple way to visualize what was covered in class. By the end of the lecture, your notes will look like a spiderweb of information with lines connecting each topic with their respective subtopics.

To use the mapping method, start by creating the topic "hubs." Each hub should be one of the major topics the course covers. From there, you'll branch out from each hub with subtopics. Below each sub-topic, make notes on relevant information covered in class. You can branch out from a sub-topic even further if you need to expand on your supporting points.

```
            Main topic
           /         \
     Sub-topic      Sub-topic
    • supporting point 1   • supporting point 1
    • supporting point 2   • supporting point 2
    • supporting point 3   • supporting point 3

     Sub-supporting
         point
    • supporting point 1
    • supporting point 2
```

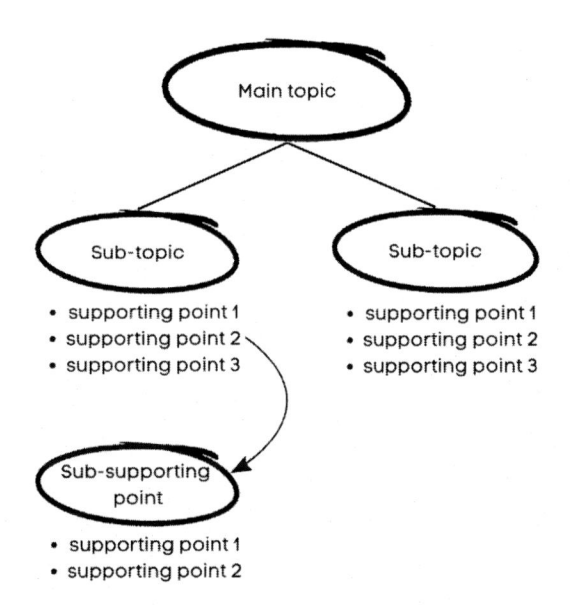

This method is not the best way to fit as much information as possible onto a page, but it's great for organizing information and topics and for illustrating the connection between subject matter.

#3: Learn How to Study

The next tool in our toolbox is **effective studying.**

Not all study time is created equal. You'll find that the more tired and distracted you are, the worse your study sessions will go. If your study time is constantly interrupted by other people, your phone, or your own intrusive thoughts, you'll never get through all the material you need to review, and you'll have twice as hard a time retaining what you do. Unproductive study sessions like this can wreak havoc on your semester. You'll begin to tire of studying, and procrastination will start looking oh-so attractive.

How can you get the most out of your study time? Well, you can implement these tips, tricks, and methods into your study routine. In the following paragraphs, we'll go over the top 5 studying tips and the top 3 studying methods.

When applied properly, these tools will help you study faster, retain more information, and leave your study sessions feeling accomplished and prepared.

Tips for Great Study Sessions

Let's start with a few tips and tricks to improve your study sessions:

1. **Get a good night's sleep.** Studying while exhausted is the perfect recipe for wasted time. Your ability to focus and your brain's capacity for critical thinking and memorization is directly correlated to how well-rested you are. One 8-hour night isn't enough, though. You need to make sure you're getting several good sleep cycles back-to-back while you prepare for an exam–especially the night before an exam.

2. **Stick with an environment that works for you.** If you have a place to go that you know is comfortable and free of distractions, why would you go anywhere else?

3. **Mimic the exam conditions.** Along those same lines, research shows that memory recall is tied to our environmental cues. The temperature, sights, sounds, and smells all quietly embed themselves

into our subconscious and associate themselves with the material you're studying. You'll have a much easier time recalling said material in the same conditions, so if you know what room your exam will be in, study in that room if possible! If not, find a room with similar conditions.

4. **Snack on smart food**. Coffee and sugar may give you a temporary boost, but the crash will leave you with regret. Rather, snack on nutrient-rich food like pretzels, nuts, or dried fruit.

5. **Silence your phone and put it in your bag or in the other room. Better yet, just turn it off and leave it at home**. Science tells us that phone use doubles as a coping mechanism. Whenever your brain feels stress, it wants to reach for something that can medicate the stress away, so it reaches for your dopamine-inducing phone. Phones are your WORST enemy when it comes to studying. Nothing is more distracting than seeing the screen light up with a little notification out of the corner of your eye. They will derail your study session faster than anything else.

Top 3 Study Methods:

Moving right along, let's go over a few effective methods of studying:

1. Active Recall

This study method uses flashcards, self-generated questions, and practice tests. It's all about repeatedly recalling something from memory. The more times you bring a memory from the back of your mind to the front, the deeper that path becomes and the easier it gets for that memory to make the journey. Simply make copies of your practice tests and retake them repeatedly. It's even better if your professor or TA posts multiple practice tests for your use. You can also take questions from your notes and make flashcards, which doubles as a chance to review your notes!

2. The Feynman Technique

The Feynman Technique was invented by famous physicist Richard Feynman. The premise behind this technique is simple: There's no better way to learn something than to teach it to a child. The technique encourages you to break every concept covered in class down into elementary terms. Could a child understand your explanation? If so, you understand it well enough yourself.

This method is a lot harder than it sounds. Children and adults essentially speak a different language. Children don't even know what questions to ask while adults have been around the block a time or two. That's what makes it such an effective study method. It forces you to study every nook and cranny of a topic until you know it forward and backward. Once you've finally gotten it simplified down to a child's level, you go back over it all again, improving and repeating your explanations.

3. The PQ4R Method

PQ4R is the acronym for this 6-step study method. This method is best used for studying long blocks of texts, like in a book:

- **Preview**: Skim through the book before reading it. Look at the illustrations, read the chapter headers, scan the headings, and read any summaries at the end of the chapters.

- **Question**: Ask yourself what you already know about the topic. What do you think will be the text's main points? Do you think this text will teach you anything new about those points?

- **Read**: Read the passage and note anything important.

- **Reflect**: Think about what you just read. How much of it did you already know? Take time to think through the things you didn't know going into the text.

- **Recite**: Talk about what you learned with somebody else, and tell them the story in your own words. Writing it all down is a good idea, too. This will improve your recall performance.

- **Review**: A week or so after completing all the steps above, return to the material and review everything you learned to further improve your recall performance.

#4: Learn How to Fight Procrastination

Sadly, the skills and methods above won't be easy to implement. Your brain and body's natural tendency toward undisciplined and lazy behavior will come out in full force. They'll fight tooth and nail to ensure you spend more time on the couch than in the library.

In other words, you'll have a strong desire to procrastinate on your studies. You must fight this. Pity the fools who wake up the day before the exam knowing they need to spend the next 24 hours cramming material they haven't reviewed in 3 months. Pity them, but don't be like them!

You can fight procrastination. All you need is to implement good habits into your routine, and you'll be golden. Use these 5 tools to help!

1. Plan Your Day in Advance

Rather than trying to figure out what needs doing next every time you finish a task, you should have a written schedule for the entire day that you can reference to save time in between tasks.

Start by obtaining a physical planner. Planners usually have a calendar as well as a note section, so they're perfect for writing down your assignments, errands, and other due dates. Then, think through your schedule from when you wake up to when you go to bed, and write it all down.

You should split your day into 3 types of tasks or goals. First, write down all the Big Things. These are your assignment due dates, study sessions, class times, project team meetings, and any other task that has to do with school. Fill in each day on your calendar with these things next.

In the remaining space, put your Everydays. Your Everydays include exercising, cooking, eating, cleaning, and alone time. Any daily hygiene-type essentials that help keep your productivity machine oiled and running smoothly go here.

Everything else goes in the remaining space. This could include an optional social event, calling to chat with your parents, or even opting for more sleep.

Write down all of these things and commit the night before to stick to the schedule. If you find it's a bit too ambitious and you get behind on sleep or on something else that shouldn't be neglected, you can rework it until it fits.

You can color code your tasks as well to help make your calendar easier to read. Categorize your tasks into groups such as urgent, important, or non-important, and assign each group a color. This way, it'll be easy to see how many urgent tasks you have and where in your day they fall. Split your day into morning, afternoon, and evening, then put your tasks in the most appropriate place and color code them accordingly.

2. Adjust Your Environment

If you're an addict, you probably shouldn't hang around places where you can effortlessly get your hands on the thing you're addicted to. The Bible talks about a similar concept in Matthew 5:29-30:

So if your eye—even your good eye—causes you to lust, gouge it out and throw it away. It is better for you to lose one part of your body than for your whole body to be thrown into hell. And if your hand—even your stronger hand—causes you to sin, cut it off and throw it away. It is better for you to lose one part of your body than for your whole body to be thrown into hell.

The principle of this passage is that we should be proactive against sin and temptation in our lives by removing ourselves from tempting situations, people, and things.

I don't know if I would call procrastination a sin, but I believe we should treat it as one. If TV causes you to get distracted and procrastinate, sell the TV and go without one. You can't watch TV if there is no TV to watch. If a friend constantly tries to chat with you during a study session, politely tell them you'd prefer not to be interrupted. If they don't stop, you can always leave. If you constantly find yourself on your phone with no memory of picking it up, leave it at home when you go to study! At the very least, turn it off and put it at the bottom of your bag.

The bottom line is that you must remove things that distract you and lead you to procrastinate in your life.

3. Keep Tasks Achievable

The larger the task, the harder it is to begin and the easier it is to procrastinate. A lot of the discomfort that leads us to procrastinate is caused by the friction involved in starting a task. It's difficult to get things rolling, but it's easy to keep them rolling.

Making your tasks smaller and easier to start can help get you over the initial hump and roll right through your tasks.

In practice, this could look like committing to studying for 30 minutes uninterrupted rather than an hour. You might dread the thought of pushing through for 60 minutes without any breaks. 30 minutes might seem challenging, yet achievable. Why wouldn't you pick the most achievable option? In other words, don't set yourself up for failure.

4. Work With Others

If you commit to studying or doing homework with a group, or if you're working on a group project, your chances of procrastinating go through the floor. That's because it's much easier to bail on yourself than to bail on other people. If you study at the library alone, nobody will wonder what's up if you don't show. If you're a part of a regular study group, they'll hold you accountable to your commitments. Those in your group will most likely keep you focused as well and check you for not paying attention or looking at your phone every other minute.

Studying with others is also a great studying hack. Having people to bounce questions off of and take turns quizzing is a huge advantage.

5. Front-Load the Worst Stuff

Do the things you like least at the beginning of the day. Just knock them out so you don't have to worry about them for the rest of the day.

This could look like working out in the morning before class if you hate working out. Or, it could look like studying before class rather than in the evening when you're already tired and not feeling like it. Whatever it is, knock it out first while your motivation and energy levels are still high.

> **Pray this Prayer**
>
> *I pray that I can work the way the Lord wants me to work in college. God, help me to work diligently toward my goals and bring glory to you in accomplishing them. Lord, give me focus during class and the discipline needed to follow these studying and note-taking techniques. Bless me with a strong memory and help me defeat procrastination.*

Chapter 3

Finding a New Church

"For where two or three are gathered in my name, there am I among them."
- Matthew 18:20

Has it occurred to you that, soon, you'll have to find a new place to call your church home? Any day now, you'll live far enough away that you won't be able to go to church with your family. In fact, for the next few months or longer, you'll probably be going to church alone. Until you find church-going friends, you'll be riding solo to Sunday morning service.

Of course, this isn't everyone's situation. Some people will be close enough to home during college to continue attending the same church. But if this doesn't describe you, and you're in the market for a new church, this chapter is written for you.

Finding a church home is vital for every Christian, but it's especially vital for young Christians. Choosing the right church with the right people can make all the difference in how strong or weak your faith becomes over the next four years. Your church community plays a big role in spiritually feeding you and keeping you accountable, but finding a church isn't always easy. It can be intimidating and awkward to walk into a new building full of people you don't know and look for some sort of connection.

Pretty tough to do in my experience, but I'm here to help! This chapter will discuss exactly what to look for in a new church, as well as a few church-hunting tips.

What Church Is

First, let's make sure we're on the same page when it comes to what church is and isn't:

1. **Church is people, not a place**. Biblically speaking, the church doesn't need a building. Well, at least not in the sense of 21st-century American church buildings. The early church met in the homes of the Apostles. Archaeologists have uncovered evidence that the Apostle Peter even built onto his home to allow for more Christians to gather.

2. **Church is for the sick and needy**. Jesus said it is the sick who need a doctor, not the healthy (Luke 5:31). If Jesus is the doctor, then the church should be the office receptionist. We are called to proclaim the Gospel and lead as many others to Christ as possible. Within our doctor analogy, the Christian's job is to ensure the doctor sees as many patients as possible.

3. **Church is for its members**. Church is by its members, for its

members. The entire point is to get as many people who come through the doors saved as possible. Old members serve new members, and when those new members begin to grow in their faith and fill service roles in the church, it'll be their turn to serve new members.

What Church Is Not

1. **Church is not a product**. Though good music, a charismatic preacher, a coffee shop in the lobby, free daycare, and sparkly clean facilities might make going to church easier and more enjoyable, those things are not what church is about. Church is not for our entertainment. If we view church as a product, we inherently think it's there to serve us. But this is the opposite of what a church is. Church only works when the members serve each other.

2. **Church is not a theological position**. Theology is the study of God and how God works. There are thousands of theologians, both dead and alive, and all have their own ideas about God and how He interacts with us and with the wider universe. Many of these ideas are not matters of faith and shouldn't be treated as such. For example, when interpreting the book of Revelation, there are countless educated guesses out there as to when Jesus will return, whether the rapture is real, and whether or not we're already in the end time. But they're just that: guesses. Guessing correctly isn't what gets you into heaven, so don't obsess over these kinds of questions.

3. **Church is not a business**. The entire point of a business is to stay

alive and keep growing. Its main concern is the satisfaction of its shareholders, not necessarily its beliefs and values. When a church becomes a business, its focus becomes pleasing the congregation. As any faithful pastor will tell you, serving others and teaching Biblical truth should be a church's primary concern, and sometimes those things actually drive members away.

How to Find a Church

Now that we agree on a few things church is and isn't, let's move on to how to find a church:

1. Decide What Church Model Interests You
As mentioned in #1 above, church is people, not a place. This means church can come in many different styles and formats depending on who makes up the church. What denomination you're looking for also makes a huge difference. Some meet on Wednesday nights, while others meet early morning on Sunday. Some churches have big buildings with high-production sound, music, and lights, while house churches meet in a living room. Some churches have been around for decades, and some are still in their planting phase.

Whichever type of church you think you'll fit best in is up to you. There is no one "right" way to model church. The only way to find out if one format is right for you over another is to visit a variety of churches.

2. Decide What You Want in a Church
Once you have an idea what type of church you'll fit in with best, you

need to lay down a few other requirements the church must meet. These requirements should be based on your values. We all hold a certain stance on things like:

- Questions of doctrine
- How a church should manage money (e.g., are they in debt?)
- Worship style
- Size
- Community involvement
- Role of women in the church

This is not an all-inclusive list, so be sure to sit down on your own and figure out what your values are.

3. Search For and Visit Churches that Interest You

Church hunting requires some leg work. You might be able to get a feel for the music or the pastor by watching a church's service online, but you won't get a feel for the people in the church. To assess the strength of a church's community, you have to visit in person if you can. So throw on your Sunday best and start sampling those pews!

4. Determine What the Church Believes

Most churches have a website listing out their specific beliefs on matters such as:

- The Trinity
- Jesus Christ
- Baptism
- Matters of salvation

- The Bible
- Communion
- Sin

If you've gone to church for long, you have a general idea of what you believe and what you don't believe on these matters. There are many small and sometimes insignificant variations of belief on these matters, which can usually be explained by what denomination the church falls under.

If you disagree with the beliefs of a church you're visiting, you probably won't be a good fit.

5. Determine if They Teach the Intent of the Bible

"Expository preaching" means teaching the content and intent of Biblical passages. Some churches only teach the Bible according to its literal word, which is sometimes useful and sometimes not. Other churches might bend passages to meet the cultural sensitivities of their congregation.

Both approaches are incomplete. Rather, a preacher's teaching should be centered on the Biblical author's intent. Teaching this way requires what's called exegetical study. Exegetics is a type of scientific study that uses the historical and cultural context of a Biblical passage, as well as linguistics to help us modern readers determine the author's original intent. Exegetics help us extract the principles out of Biblical passages that make no sense on their face to our modern ears.

Using what we learn about the intent of Biblical passages from exegetical studies, we can then form sound doctrine. Doctrine is the interpretation of a passage of the Bible shared by scholarly or other authoritative church sources. One example of Christian doctrine is the teaching of baptism. Even though different denominations practice baptism differently, all practice it. That's because the vast majority of authoritative sources agree on the importance of baptism based on their studies of the texts that make up the Bible.

If a church doesn't conduct expository preaching, you should consider crossing them off your list and moving on to the next church. But this means you need to know your stuff, too. You can't know if a preacher isn't teaching the Bible's intent if you've never read it and researched it for yourself. Habitually studying the Word should be a cornerstone of your faith. If you don't learn the Bible's lessons for yourself, you'll always depend on the interpretation of others. Therefore, your faith will never really be your own.

6. Determine Their Heart for Service

Serving others in some form is non-negotiable for churches. The Bible is very clear on how churches should treat the needy:

"And the King will answer them, 'Truly, I say to you, as you did it to one of the least of these, my brothers, you did it to me.'"

• Matthew 25:40

As each has received a gift, use it to serve one another, as good stewards of God's varied grace.

• 1 Peter 4:10

"For even the Son of Man came not to be served but to serve, and to give his life as a ransom for many."

• Mark 10:45

These verses and many others make the church's expectation of serving others crystal clear.

If a church you're visiting doesn't at least give a portion of offerings to local and international missions, you should probably move on to the next church. If a church you're visiting doesn't serve the physical, spiritual, or economic needs of its congregation, you should probably move on to another church. If a church you're visiting doesn't plan or host mission trips for its members, shake the dust from your feet (Matthew 10:14) and move on to the next one.

7.   Do They Offer Programs You Need?

Some churches have enough resources to offer an expanse of programs and classes. Many churches in a college town will even have programs specific to college kids. These can be activities like small groups, service groups, Sunday school classes, or virtual classes.

If you are interested in these types of programs, then make sure the churches you're visiting provide them. Not all of them do.

I highly recommend finding a church with a variety of small group options, whether it's a Sunday school class or a weekday gathering. They're a great way to meet friends and begin building your Christian community.

> **Pray this Prayer**
> *Lord, help me connect with a solid church of believers in my new college town. Place me in a community where I can flourish and my faith and intellect can grow. Lord, help me to keep my priorities straight when searching for a new church and remember what church is and isn't.*

Chapter 4

Finding New Friends

"There are "friends" who destroy each other, but a real friend sticks closer than a brother."

- Colossians 3:23-24

"Friend" is one of the worst words in the English language.

That's a strong statement, I know. But I think it's true because "Friend" doesn't really mean anything in the way we use it. In our everyday use of the word, a friend could mean someone you've known and loved your entire life, or it could mean someone you get along with at work. What good is a word that could apply to both?

The word "love" in English has the same problem. The Greeks have 6 words for love in their language. They have *"eros,"* which means sexual passion. They have *"philia,"* which means deep friendship. *"Ludos"* means playful love, *"agape"* means love for everyone, *"pragma"* means long-standing love, and *"philautia"* means love of the self. But in English? The single word "love" could be used in all 6 of those contexts.

We English speakers simply don't have enough words to describe the complex relationships we form with people. Do you think this means native English speakers have a shallow comprehension of friendship and love? If so, how does our shallow conceptualization of friendship compare to the way the Bible talks about friendship? Let's dig into that.

What Does the Bible Say About Friendship?

Some think we don't choose our friends but that they simply happen to be in our lives. They believe our friends aren't our friends because they have superb friendship qualities or are especially suited to be our friends. They're only our friends because they happen to be near us.

What do you think of this notion? Do you think you really have any say in who your friends are?

That certainly isn't what the Bible teaches.

According to the Bible, not only do we choose our friends, but it matters which friends we choose. That's because Biblical friendship is all about improving each other, holding each other accountable, and sacrificing for each other. This is encapsulated nicely in Proverbs 27:17:

> *As iron sharpens iron, so a friend sharpens a friend.*

Old-school theologian Adam Clarke wrote a great commentary on this verse back in the early 1800s. We're digging deep for this wisdom!

Clarke says that the author of Proverbs is most likely referring to the mind when he says, *"A friend sharpens a friend."* Friends don't primarily make us physically stronger. They might help, especially when we need a spot in the gym. But we can get physically stronger on our own. What friends really do is help us sharpen our intellect and character.

Having someone–a friend–who causes you to reflect on your life, choices, and behavior is greatly valuable. So rarely do we self-reflect on our own. It usually takes someone asking a question or pointing out something we've done to prompt us to consider our ethics.

Friends force us to dive deeply into our beliefs. A friend–especially a Christian friend–will want to get to know you and what you believe. This curiosity will cause them to ask you questions about your beliefs, which in turn will force you to think about and articulate them if you can. A friend might show you that you don't understand something you strongly believe as well as you thought you did.

And so, you become sharper.

6 Traits to Look for in a Godly Friend

Motivational speaker Jim Rohn once said, *"You are the average of the five people you spend the most time with."* By this, he means we tend to adopt the likes, dislikes, and behaviors of the people we hang around.

Interestingly, the Bible says the same thing. Take a look at Proverbs 13:20:

> *Walk with the wise and become wise;*
> *associate with fools and get in trouble.*

Then there's 1 Corinthians 15:33:

> *"Don't be fooled by those who say such things, for "bad company corrupts good character."*

When we're around people often enough, we become just like them. Perhaps this is why we all eventually become our parents! You probably hate to hear it now, but you'll realize someday it's true.

1. They're Believers.

Obviously, the first thing to look for in a Godly friend is whether they're a believer to begin with. We'll skip over this point because most of the people you want to be friends with won't be shy about telling you they're Christians.

The following traits, however, will be a little harder to sniff out. Some just take time to determine whether the person has them or not. Others require that you imagine the person in a variety of scenarios. Of course, the more you hang out with them, the more you'll learn!

2. Capable of Forgiveness

Forgiveness is often misconstrued as a magical word that resolves problems between people. Just say the magic phrase, *"I forgive you,"* and *whoosh!* You and the other person are totally reconciled as if nothing ever happened.

That's not at all how forgiveness works. That's a better description for *forbearance*. Forbearance means forgetting, excusing, or otherwise ignoring something that bothers you. Forbearance is necessary. Without it, we'd turn into thin-skinned children who can't take a joke. We need to be able to brush aside small slights, such as someone accidentally interrupting you, a harmless joke at your expense, an annoying coworker's constant sniffle, or getting cut off in traffic.

Forgiveness, on the other hand, is meant for offenses that cannot be ignored or forgotten. If someone steals from you, physically harms you, or sabotages you, these actions require discussion and time for resolution to take place. They also require consequences. Nothing about forgiveness implies that consequences, legal or otherwise, should be foregone.

The end goal of the forgiveness process is for your heart to no longer hold a grudge toward the person or feel they owe you anything. If the other person is remorseful and willing to correct their actions, we should let them in and allow the relationship to be restored with no grudges intact.

Even if the other person skates by with no consequences, shows no remorse, or takes zero steps toward repentance, we still have the ability to let it all go. The emotional pain caused by their actions is ours, not theirs. It's up to us what we do with it. We can choose to be prideful and hold onto it because we *deserve* an apology that may never come, or we can shake the dust from our feet and move on with our lives (Matthew 10:14).

This is an important skill to look for in a Godly friend. People will always disappoint us, and we will always disappoint others. It can't be helped. Be sure to surround yourself with friends who are willing to accept your repentance, drop their grudges, and move forward in the relationship.

3. Integrity

Integrity is how you act when no one is looking. The Hebrew word for integrity is sometimes translated as *"uprightness."* In scripture, someone who is upright is someone who faithfully adheres to God's law. Outside of scripture, uprightness can mean adherence to a moral or religious code. Either way, an upright person is someone who follows the rules no matter what. This means that one understanding of the concept of integrity is strictly sticking to what we claim to believe.

An alternative meaning for integrity is strength. Engineers and builders use integrity when referring to the strength of a material or the structural soundness of a building.

We want to look for friends who have both kinds of integrity. We want to be friends with people who won't talk about us or double-cross us behind our backs. We want to be friends with people who we can trust will do the right thing, and we want friends who do the right things for the right reasons. We want friends who will take responsibility for there actions, who will tell the truth even when it may harm their reputation. We want to be this kind of person as well!

We also want friends who are strong. As we talked about earlier, friends sharpen each other. We should surround ourselves with tough people who aren't going to break during the sharpening process.

All in all, it comes down to trust. High-integrity people are also highly trustworthy people. High-integrity people are also high-endurance and high-patience people. If you can trust that someone will do the right thing and won't collapse under the pressures of life, then you want that person as a friend. Seeing someone express gratitude to others and show respect to themselves and those around them are traits of those who have integrity.

One simple thing you can look for when determining someone's integrity is to observe how they treat homeless people and people in the service industry. If someone is rude or dismissive to the homeless, waiters, custodians, and bus drivers, they are a low-integrity person, and you should avoid them.

4. Honesty

Liars will waste your time and drive you crazy. Just don't deal with them. Love them, but don't spend time with them. Take note of the times you catch people lying about little things like who was in line first or if they find something and don't return it. If people are willing to lie about little things, they'll probably be comfortable lying about big things as well.

They'll likely be really good at lying about the big things because they've had so much practice lying about the little things!

As with integrity, honest people take responsibility for their actions and tell the truth even when it may harm their reputation. While honesty may feel uncomfortable, it will benefit your relationship in the long run.

5. Holds You Accountable

True friends bring our sins to light and tell us the hard truth, even when we don't want to hear it. If we're falling short more than usual, a Godly friend will be there to gracefully explain the error of our ways and encourage us to repent and be better. But they won't just leave it there. A Godly friend will be by our side during our struggle with sin.

6. A Heart for Service

Serving others is one of the most important tenets of the Christian faith. What did Jesus do right before the culminating event of his life (the crucifixion)? He washed his disciples' feet! Do you realize how significant that was? Not only was foot washing reserved for slaves in Jesus's time, but it was reserved for the lowest of slaves. It was one of the worst tasks you could be assigned because of how filthy people's feet got back then.

Jesus, the son of God, stooped to the status of the lowliest servant to make the point that no follower of Jesus is above serving others. The closest modern-day comparison I can think of is the Pope cleaning toilets at a prison.

If a person has a heart for service, you know two things about them:

- **They don't think they're better than anyone else**. Whether it's the homeless, the poor, or the incarcerated, no one is above another in the eyes of Jesus. This is a difficult realization to reach, but it's a sure sign of a mature and Godly friend.

- **They take their faith seriously**. Serving others requires sacrifice. It requires your time, your energy, your money, and stepping out of your comfort zone. Only people who take faith seriously are willing to make those sacrifices.

Why do you care if your friend has a heart for service? Because all Christians should have a heart for service, and if you don't, a friend who does could help you get there. Steel sharpens steel!

Where to Meet Godly Friends

Now that you know what to look for in a Godly friend—and how to *be* a Godly friend—let's talk about where you can find these people.

Church seems like the obvious answer, right? While church is certainly a great place to meet other Christians (this applies to dating as well as making friends), it isn't the only option. Perhaps it isn't even your best option.

I don't know if you've noticed, but church is a structured activity. It starts at the same time every week, the regulars sit in the same pews every week, the same people speak every week, and the same songs are usually played every week. It's a repetitive, organized event that keeps moving no matter what.

Does that sound like a great environment for making friends, especially at your young age? You might strike up a conversation with someone in the lobby over coffee and a donut. But as soon as the service starts, you'll part ways and may or may not see each other after service. So, what other options are there for meeting Christians?

Well, since you're in college, there are plenty! There are likely dozens of Christian groups and clubs on your campus; you just have to find them. Below are some common groups you'll find on most campuses in the US.

Most of these groups encourage member outreach and ministry to the rest of campus. They aren't just hangout sessions for people who are already Christians, but they can double as a group to evangelize with.

1. InterVarsity Christian Fellowship

InterVarsity's goal is to create on-campus communities of undergraduates, graduates, and faculty equipped to share the Gospel. You can sign up to join one of the

InterVarsity also encourages its members to participate in global missions. Through their missions program, you could have the opportunity to study abroad. This program can even count for credit hours, depending on your university.

2. Cru

Cru (which is short for Campus Crusade for Christ) is one of the largest student ministries in the nation. They offer small groups (weekly gatherings that are similar to church but more laid back) and also train members in discipleship and evangelism. Their overall goal is to bring more college students to Christ. Visit www.cru.org/us/en/locator/campus to see if your campus has a Cru chapter.

3. The Navigators

The Navigators is heavily focused on discipleship, which they define as helping others grow in their relationship with Christ. They encourage discipleship through their Life-to-Life program, which matches students with a fellow Navigator and gives communities using this link: https://intervarsity.org/signupnows you the opportunity to build a Christ-centered and evangelism-focused relationship with them. You can learn more about The Navigators and their Life-to-Life program by visiting their website: https://www.navigators.org/life-to-life/?sf_ac=w07

4. Alpha

Alpha is a 12-week video series focused on evangelizing to non-Christians or new Christians. The videos break down Christian concepts into everyday language and discuss common questions and objections people have about Christianity. You may have a hard time finding an Alpha group on your campus because the organization is smaller and is more popular in Europe. That's okay because you can start your own! Alpha is free to set up, and all the course material is free. You can learn more at alphausa.org.

> **Pray this Prayer**
> *Lord, help me find friends who can bring me closer to you. Connect me with friends who will sharpen me in my faith and many other ways. Put me in places where I can meet the people I should be spending my time with, Lord, and help me to gracefully manage the friendships I should end.*

Chapter 5

Dating

"Therefore a man shall leave his father and his mother and hold fast to his wife, and they shall become one flesh."

- Genesis 2:24

We've covered platonic relationships. But what about the… non-platonic type? Yes, I'm talking about romantic relationships. I don't want you to get anxious. Even if you were unsuccessful with the lads and ladies in high school, college is a blank slate. It's a chance for you to reinvent yourself.

Let's be clear about one thing: The following pages talk about dating in terms of dating to marry. This is when you date with the end goal of marriage in mind. Dating to marry means you know your deal-breakers and have a general idea of what type of person you want to be with. You don't date to sleep around or just have fun. Feel free to date around, of course. How else are you going to find the person you'll marry? But for every person you date, you should be asking throughout the relationship, *"Is this someone I could marry?"*

It also means you part ways with people who have deal-breakers. Don't waste their time by continuing the relationship even when you know it inevitably must end. Even if it's hard, part ways with people who just aren't a fit, because that's what it means to marry.

Deciding Your Deal-Breakers

With that in mind, what are your deal-breakers? Have you thought of those? Are they the same as in high school? It's vital you know what they are, so let's go over some common ones:

- Having kids or not
- Spends too freely
- Spends too tightly
- Different political beliefs
- Too stubborn
- Too flexible
- How free time is spent
- Core religious beliefs

While these don't have to be *your* deal-breakers, they're nonetheless important questions you should be asking your partner.

How do you decide what your deal breakers are? Well, some of them are and should come naturally to you. You'll know them in your gut. These will usually be matters of attraction—the things about a person that catch your attention in the first place. Is it the way they do their hair? Their height? Their eyes or their smile? What I'm getting at is this: Attraction can be a deal-breaker. It's not shallow or vain to admit it. If you're not attracted to the person, you probably won't go the distance.

Attraction is not just a shallow, surface-level metric, though. It encompasses way more than just someone's physical looks. It's largely about their personality and overall "vibe," if you will. Attraction is affected by someone's sense of humor, quirks, cute flaws, and overall disposition. True attraction should mean you're friends with a person and also think they're hot. How could you spend the rest of your life with someone who is anything but that?

Being attracted to someone is not the only deal-breaker that matters. It's just one piece of the puzzle. Next are the deal-breakers other than lack of attraction. These are the ones that require a little more time in thought and some soul-searching. You'll have to sit down and put in the effort to think through these deal-breakers. In fact, you should do just that. Grab a pen, a piece of paper, and a seat, and let's work out what your deal-breakers are.

Family counselors often say the 3 things couples fight over the most are money, sex, and in-laws. These are 3 great deal-breakers you should consider. Let's start with money.

First deal-breaker: How do you feel about money?

It's important to know how your partner views and treats money. Disagreeing on money can not only lead to fights and tension in your marriage, but it can also lead to huge boundary crossings and an overall erosion of trust.

Some of us are savers, and some of us are spenders. There's nothing wrong with being either one as long as your lifestyle isn't beyond your means, but when the savers and spenders get together, things tend to get a little bumpy. So, it's necessary to know which one your potential partner is.

While it would be nice to agree on everything about savings goals and spending habits with your potential partner, it's not like your marriage will fail if you don't. Spenders and savers can make it work together. It just takes a lot of extra effort.

What's more important to find out is whether the person has any attitudes toward money that amount to a character flaw. You'll meet some people like this in life who just can't figure out how to plan their finances. They spend too much, make too little, put it all on credit cards, take out payday loans, buy stupid stuff, and give money to other people for no good reason. Have you ever seen Family Guy? Peter Griffin is a great representation of this type of person.

Being with someone like this is not a cross you want to carry. In the worst-case scenario, these types of people make financial decisions that put their families at risk. They do things like borrow against their home, invest life savings into dumb inventions, gamble away college funds, or worse. You'll save yourself a lot of heartache if you put Peter Griffin on your deal-breaker list.

Second deal-breaker: How do you feel about sex?

Some might say this is an inappropriate topic for a book aimed at college students, but I disagree. For one, I'm not going to play dumb. I know kids of all backgrounds and beliefs have sex in high school. Whether you were a heartbreaker in high school or you stayed abstinent, sex is probably something you'll experience eventually, whether it's before or after marriage. Therefore, it's something you should consider.

Also, you've presumably gone through puberty already and have been in touch with your body for a few years now. You're well aware that sex is a natural biological urge. Why shouldn't you consider your preferences, likes, dislikes, and boundaries concerning something your body already wants to do? To me, this is a healthy topic of discussion for those leaving their teenage years.

Sex, in the right context, is greatly celebrated in the Bible. Just read Proverbs 5:15-19 to see how the Bible illustrates sex:

> *Drink water from your own cistern, running water from your own well.*
> *Should your springs overflow in the streets, your streams of water in the public squares?*
> *Let them be yours alone, never to be shared with strangers.*
> *May your fountain be blessed, and may you rejoice in the wife of your youth.*
> *A loving doe, a graceful deer—may her breasts satisfy you always, may you ever be intoxicated with her love.*

This passage emphasizes the beauty of a monogamous relationship in a time when few men of means were monogamous. At the time Proverbs was written, a high number of wives was seen as an indicator of great status. The more wives you had, the richer and more powerful you were.

Notice that the author doesn't disapprove of sex, just sex with multiple partners. In fact, the author uses poetic, beautiful language to describe it. In the last verse, they even use the word "love" interchangeably with sex. This leads us to believe that this Biblical author had a favorable view of sex within their religious context (Judaism).

For these reasons, we're going to talk about sex as a deal-breaker.

For the purposes of this book, there are two deal-breakers when it comes to sex: Frequency and whether or not you're going to wait till marriage.

Let's discuss the merits of waiting until marriage:

1. Waiting till marriage is the traditional Biblical interpretation. Although some debate has popped up in certain circles about this stance, most Christians throughout time have viewed sex outside of marriage as a sin.

2. Waiting until marriage is the responsible thing to do. Even if you disagree that sex outside of marriage is a sin, waiting is still undisputedly the responsible thing to do. There's no quicker way to

derail your college career than an unplanned pregnancy, and there's no better way to ruin your semester–or even your life–than catching an STD.

Whichever path you choose, just make sure you're careful.

Next, let's talk about frequency. How often you desire to have sex is known as your sex drive, or your libido. Libido is your motivation or desire to behave sexually. It can vary from preferences and life circumstances.

The consensus is that there is no such thing as a "normal" sex drive. Everyone's libido varies depending on several factors such as age, health, stress, social issues, past experiences, and hormone levels. These hormones that affect the libido include testosterone and estrogen, and neurotransmitters like dopamine. These hormones help regulate the libido and develop a biological urge for sex.

Frequency is the only aspect of sex that's worthwhile talking about before marriage. Honestly, everything else will figure itself out. Ask a couple with 30 years of marriage under their belt, and they'll say they eventually found what works for them. However, having a sex drive conflicting with your spouses can lead to some serious relationship problems. In fact, according to Psychology Today, frequency is the number one sex-related argument between married couples.

In this *Psychology Today* article, the author says that disagreeing on sex frequency leads to a battle of needs. When high-desire partners ask for sex and get turned down, it can often feel like rejection. This feeling of rejection then devolves into feelings of anger, inadequacy, or confusion and the low-desire partner will notice and feel it. The low-desire partner will rarely respond with more sex. Counter-productively, they'll usually respond with less sex, because no one is turned on by an angry partner or unwanted sexual pressure.

This dynamic spirals until it's nearly impossible for either partner to get what they desire. The low-drive partner will say, *"I'd want to have sex if you didn't get upset every time we talk about it."* The high-drive partner will respond with, *"I wouldn't be so upset if we had more sex."* Can you see how this cycle would be difficult to escape? There isn't much you can do about it.

For the most part, our libido is our libido. You can't just wake up and change it. It ebbs and flows on its own over the years, and you can do small things to influence it in a more favorable direction, such as working out and eating healthy. But rarely will two polar opposites on the libido spectrum ever find a way to meet in the middle. Sadly, many marriages are ruined by this problem. Some of these marriages work it out with honest, clear communication and patience.

In the digital age, we're often exposed to pornography even if we don't seek it out for ourselves. The reality is that pornography can quickly become an addiction and effect libido in ways that contribute to unhealthy relationships or self-image.

How do you find out someone's sex drive without having sex with them? It's really simple. You ask! Even if the other person is a virgin or hasn't had a lot of experience, they still know how much they think about or want to engage in sexual behavior. Those thoughts and feelings are a great indicator of their libido. If someone naturally desires sex just as often as you, they could make for a great match!

Third deal-breaker: How do you feel about in-laws?

This is a question you aren't at all equipped to answer right now. At 18 or 19 years old, you have no idea what having in-laws is going to be like. Trust me, they have a huge effect on your marriage.

Let me catch you up and go over a few things that matter in reference to in-laws. Here are some questions to ask when exploring the topic of in-laws with a potential partner:

1. How much time do you want to spend with your parents?
If you're in a relationship, and you've met your partner's parents, then you have a general idea of how easy they are to get along with. You might know by now whether they're funny or annoying, pleasant or pushy, and whether being around them is a positive or negative experience.

Depending on how well you click with your potential in-laws, spending too much time with them might be a dealbreaker for you. It could also be the case that your partner is put off by you spending too much time or talking too much with their parents. Maybe that's their dealbreaker.

Before deciding if your partner has an in-law dealbreaker, you first need to estimate how much time you can really expect to spend with your potential in-laws. Here are some questions you can ask to help find an answer:

- Does their family have a group chat? If so, you'll be added to it once you're married or even before.
- How often does your partner talk to their parents? If it's every day, you can expect to talk to their parents every day or at least hear about the conversation.
- How often does their family get together? Whether it's for a birthday, anniversary, or other occasion, once you're married, you are your spouse's permanent plus one.
- Do their parents ever "drop in" on your partner or their siblings? If so, this will likely continue into your marriage.

2. Whose side are you on?

The Bible says in Genesis 2:24 that man will *"leave his father and mother"* and become *"one flesh"* with his wife. This language illustrates that marriage supersedes all other relationships, even blood ones. If you're one flesh, you have no choice but to prioritize your wife. Where one goes, so goes the other. When one struggles or hurts, so does the other. Once married, the man has new blood to whom he owes his life above all else.

Even though the text says *"man,"* it's accepted and understood that this Biblical principle applies to women as well. Women are also to leave their mother and father and become one flesh with their husbands. That's logically how it has to work, as a husband can't become one flesh with a wife who's unwilling to become one flesh with her husband.

Sharing this understanding of marriage is vital for its success. You both must understand that the other now comes first, and the family of origin comes second. This can lead to some uncomfortable, sad, and upsetting situations, like missing a wedding to go to a funeral, or vice versa. Your future spouse must understand that one set of in-laws will sometimes be put before the other. When this happens, in-laws will be upset and want to lay blame. You and your spouse must approach the conflict as a team. It's you two versus the problem, not you versus your spouse versus the problem. Or even worse, you versus your spouse and in-laws.

Similarly, you and your future spouse must understand the importance of saving face. Saving face is an idiom that means allowing someone to maintain their self-respect. In the context of marriage, it means taking your spouse's side in an argument with their parents or other family, even if you think they're wrong. It means never rebuking (criticizing, condemning, or otherwise correcting their behavior) in public, but only in private. It doesn't matter how embarrassing or inappropriate your spouse is behaving; save your rebuke for home.

Of course, this isn't the case for violence. You should absolutely intervene in a safe manner as soon as possible if your spouse displays signs of violence, aggression, or abuse.

Fourth question: How do you feel about kids?

This is a huge should-be deal-breaker many couples overlook. Sometimes, people are ambivalent about kids before getting into a serious relationship. They don't care either way. When these people inevitably change their minds and decide either that they do want kids or don't want kids, things can get sticky depending on their partner's position.

Do you think you want kids, or are you undecided? You have plenty of time to think about this sort of thing, but you *should* be thinking about it.

"Wait, I don't have any kids. So how could I know if I want them or not?" This is a great point and another unfair decision society puts at the feet of young people. Regardless of how fair or unfair it is, it's a question you have to answer, and you don't have forever to answer it. Let me fill you in a bit on what comes with kids. Then, you can decide if it sounds like something you want to embark on:

Having kids is a two-sided coin. On one side, they're what you love most in life. You would die for them if you had to, and you want to give them anything and everything you can. You have endless dreams and ideas of what they'll be like and what they'll become as adults. Kids are a fulfilling adventure that far outweighs the cost. Being a parent can become the most memorable work you will ever do. You're taking part in God's commandment to multiply and replenish the earth, bringing the greatest joy and reward.

On the other side, kids are a nightmare. When they're infants, they require constant attention. You have to be with them every second they're not sleeping. They never sleep through the night, which wrecks your sleep schedule and slowly drains the life from you. When they're toddlers, they make a scene every time you're in public. They throw fits in restaurants and have breakdowns in the back seat of the car just outside of arm's reach. Then, once they're teenagers, they forget all about the diapers you changed and decide they hate you. They never talk to you, and they're annoyed every time you speak to them.

This is the worst-case scenario, though. You get my point.

Having kids is always said to be one of the most fulfilling things you can do, but it does require a lot of sacrifice. Are you willing to make that sacrifice? That's something you'll have to decide.

These are not all the deal-breakers you should have. There are plenty more. This is just a primer to get you thinking about those things. Feel free to add to your list as you learn more about yourself.

4 Things to Look For in a Godly Partner

If your deal-breakers are the things you *don't* want in a partner, this list is of things you *do* want in a partner.

This list covers more than just matters of faith. There are many practical things to look for in someone. If someone has a strong faith, great! But a major flaw can make it irrelevant when pursuing a relationship with that person.

1. Attributes of a Godly Friend:

To start this list, let's quickly go back over the things to look for in a Godly friend:
- Faith
- Forgiveness
- Integrity
- Honesty
- Accountability
- Heart for service

I'm repeating these because they all apply to romantic relationships as well. For the same reasons you want Godly friends with these qualities, you want a Godly partner with these qualities. I won't spell the reasons back out in detail. Just reread the last chapter if you need a refresher.

2. Committed to Growing in their Relationship with Christ

Anyone your age who thinks there isn't room for improvement when it comes to their faith should immediately trigger a red flag. There is always room for improvement; that's part of what defines Christianity. To be a Christian means you strive to be like Christ. Christ was perfect, and we'll never be perfect, so there is always room for growth. Faith is all about being committed to the process of shedding our worldly selves and becoming as Christ-like as possible.

Your spouse should feel the same way. This old 2000s-era youth group illustration explains why:

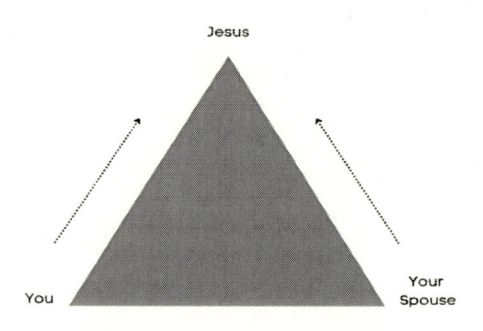

```
                        Jesus
                         /\
                        /  \
                       /    \
                      /      \
                     /        \
                    /          \
                   /            \
                  /              \
                 /                \
                /                  \
               You              Your
                                Spouse
```

As you can see, when you and your spouse both pursue Jesus, you inevitably and progressively get closer to each other. A mutual pursuit of Christ is one of the best things a relationship can have. It keeps the focus pointed toward something bigger than itself.

You want to ensure your future spouse shares this pursuit of Christ because, if they don't, you'll leave them behind at the bottom of the pyramid. As you move forward in holiness, they'll remain stagnant. One day, you'll wake up and discover you're in two totally different places faith-wise. It's best to avoid this scenario altogether and ensure you and your future spouse are equally zealous and committed to growth in

Christ.

This is what Paul is referring to in 2 Corinthians 6:14 when he says we should be "equally yoked" with our partners:

Do not be unequally yoked with unbelievers. For what partnership has righteousness with lawlessness? What fellowship has light with darkness?

A yoke is a wooden bar joining two oxen at the neck, forcing them to work together when pulling a plow. If a team of oxen are unequally yoked, one will end up doing more than their share of the work. The disparate workload will take a toll on both oxen, one suffering from being overworked while other becomes apathetic. If you and your spouse are unequally yoked in your faith, the same will happen, and your proverbial fields will be overgrown with weeds, unevenly plowed, and one of you will always feel exhausted and taken advantage of.

3. Has Control of Their Pride

The Oxford Dictionary defines pride as "a feeling of a deep pleasure derived from one's own achievements." This definition highlights the positive connotation pride sometimes carries. In our previous chapter on work, we talked about taking pride in your work and in your accomplishments. Nothing wrong at all with this type of pride!

But pride has a negative connotation as well. The negative side is defined by self-centeredness. When our pride runs away from us, it has deadly effects on our character. It turns us into arrogant knuckleheads and causes us to close our ears to advice, shut our eyes to the examples of others, and refuse to accept feedback.

People who have control of their pride are much better suited for marriage than those who don't. They're better at handling interpersonal conflict as well as the difficulties of life. If or when you get married, you'll see this first hand. People who can't get past their pride can't admit they're wrong, made a mistake, or failed. They make up excuses, double down, deny, get defensive, redirect, and never learn from the past. This type of attitude will destroy a marriage. Marriage requires grace and humility, two things people with out-of-control pride don't have.

People with runaway pride also have a hard time managing life's struggles. They poorly handle obstacles when they appear. They think they're superior to others and shouldn't struggle in the same ways. When they inevitably find out they do struggle as others do, they blame others for their problems. These types of people are extremely hard to work with, and you should avoid them in a partnership.

You'll know prideful people when you see them because they love talking about themselves, put down others to benefit themselves, never admit they're wrong or apologize, and can't handle criticism. They also can't laugh at themselves. This is not the type of person to consider for marriage.

4. Willing to Make Sacrifices
Whether you like it or not, life comes with tradeoffs. We simply don't

have enough time or energy to accomplish everything we want to accomplish. Because of this, we have to figure out how to prioritize our time.

Marriage is no exception to this rule. If anything, it's more important to have your priorities straight in marriage than anywhere else. Creating a good marriage requires time and intentional effort. Your spouse will want to spend time with you, and you'll hopefully want to spend time with your spouse. Maintaining your relationship means lazy nights on the couch, date nights, weekend sleep-ins, vacations, and small acts of service. All of these things are way more time-consuming than they sound.

When kids arrive on the scene, your time becomes even more precious. The minutes and hours of your day get chopped up and divided, sometimes in a way you don't like and can't control. If you choose to prioritize your family, your career, friendships, interests, and hobbies will suffer. This is the nature of trade-offs.

Additionally, it's a double-edged sword. Not only will you have less time to put toward these things, but you'll have less energy as well, meaning the time you will have to work will be less productive. It's just how the human body works. We aren't computers capable of perfect and complete effort into everything we do.

It's in your best interest to pursue relationships with people who are capable of making sacrifices regarding their time, their other relationships, and their career aspirations. You don't want to be married to someone who chooses friends or work over family. Of course, friends and work are important and shouldn't be neglected. But family comes first, and those around you should know it. If someone isn't willing to make that prioritization, then don't date them.

> **Pray this Prayer**
> *Lord, help me keep my priorities straight when dating. Help me to stand by my deal-breakers and to put love first, not lust. Give me the strength to walk away from relationships that aren't good for me or that aren't focused on you. God, guide me in deciding what I value and what my deal-breakers may be. Keep me principled, Lord, and make me a partner that deserves a Godly partner.*

Chapter 6

Mental Health

"For to set the mind on the flesh is death, but to set the mind on the Spirit is life and peace."

- Romans 8:6

This might sound crazy, but mental health is a fairly new concept. Only within the last few decades has the importance of caring for our mental health been communicated to the public. The term "mental health" was never used by the medical community until 1946. Before then, they used a similar concept called "mental hygiene." Mental hygiene did not mean back then what mental health means to us today. Then, mental hygiene practices included "cures" such as lobotomies. In fact, in 1949, the inventor of the lobotomy won the Nobel Prize for Medicine.

Older generations simply didn't understand the mind or the mind-body connection. The mind-body connection is the idea that there's a link between your thoughts, feelings, and attitudes and your physical health, and vice versa. Scientists who study the mind-body connection have come to realize the two-way relationship between our emotions and our body. They've also come to understand that we can't always control or even recognize our emotions and the hormones associated with them.

Many thoughts and feelings happen without our conscious knowledge—whether we want them to happen or not. Your body and your brain often instinctively react in ways that don't make sense, storing stress and trauma and developing triggers without you even knowing it, meaning our brains and bodies sometimes respond beyond our control.

Emotions are similar to the weather. Everyone's brain has a unique climate, where emotions range in intensity and duration. Just as it's important to know the warning signs of inclement weather and how to prepare for a severe storm, we can gauge our emotions to take safety precautions when in a crisis.

Without an understanding of the mind-body connection and that our brain and body are not always under our control, we end up living without any compassion for those struggling with mental health.

We see this all throughout history. Your grandparents and their grandparents were born in an age when depression was viewed as a weakness rather than a disorder. During the Great Depression, suicides skyrocketed as people failed to cope with the stress. During World War One, troops could face the firing squad for "cowardice" when they froze or refused to leave their dugout and storm no man's land when the brain-scrambling effects of shell shock left them twitching without any control over their body.

These generations thought the mind was 100% in their control, and if your mind had a problem, it was because you were too soft, too lazy, or had poor character. They believed it was within their control to just turn the depression or shell shock off. Thankfully, we now know that isn't how it works. We now understand the brain's complexity and the importance of developing healthy habits that promote a healthy mind.

Keeping Tabs on Your Mental Health

There are many facets to mental health, including stress, anxiety, self-esteem, depression, and more. All of these facets need their due share of attention.

In the following section, I'll lay out how to manage each facet. Mental health is not something you can just cure once and for all. Good mental health is more of a process than a destination. Because of this, it will ebb and flow throughout life. As life throws obstacles in your way, these management tips will help you keep the scales tipping toward adequate mental health.

#1: Stress

There will be no shortage of stressful moments throughout your college career. Whether you're in the middle of another sleep-deprived study session, cramming the night before an exam, or furiously scribbling in as many answers on the test as you can before time's up, your body and mind are going to get stressed out.

It is incredibly important to manage your stress. If you don't, you could be at greater risk for developing long-term problems such as high blood pressure, heart disease, and a weakened immune system. Managing your stress starts with knowing how your body and mind react to stressors. Here are some common signs of being over-stressed:

- Physical:
  - You can't relax without alcohol or another substance
  - You have persistent headaches
  - It's hard to stop yourself from overeating
  - Pain in the chest or a racing heart
  - Stomach problems
  - Trouble sleeping

- Emotional:
  - General sad or lethargic feeling
  - Panic attacks
  - Depression
  - Anxiety or irritability

Once you know your stress symptoms and figure out what triggers them, you can then recognize the signs and know when to activate your stress management techniques.

Here are some techniques for managing stress:

1. Change Your Body, Change Your Mind

A healthy body goes a long way toward fostering a healthy mind. Exercise has long been a proven way to expend stress from the body. Physical activity releases endorphins, which can have mood-boosting effects. In addition, stress has many physical symptoms, and being in good physical shape can help mitigate some of those symptoms.

You don't have to hit the weights or go for a jog to use physical activity to relieve stress. Sometimes, just going on a walk can do the trick. There are other low-impact exercises you can do such as stretching, push-ups, jumping jacks, or walking a flight of stairs. The idea is that doing some sort of physical activity can take your mind off of whatever you're stressing about.

2. Maintain Sleep Hygiene

Sleep hygiene means having a bedtime environment and an evening routine that promotes deep, uninterrupted sleep. Good sleep hygiene helps you to fall asleep faster, stay asleep throughout the night, and sleep deeper. Getting back-to-back nights of this type of sleep is one of the best ways to manage your physical and mental health.

When used correctly, good sleep hygiene can help you create and maintain a consistent sleep routine.

3. Take Time to Decompress

"Decompress" means to unwind or to relax. It's something we all need to do near the end of the day as we're getting ready for bed. How many people do you know who can go straight from work to sleep? No, most of us need some time in between to eat, drink, watch TV, or just veg around with friends and family.

You can also decompress in between tasks, not just at the end of the day. Not only will this help lower your stress levels, but it can also aid in memory retention. Several studies have shown the benefits of quiet rest, or even sleep, right after learning new information. Doing so can help build synapse pathways and form better, clearer memories.

4. Hunt the Good Stuff

This is the only stress management tip I'll list here having to do with your attitude. All the others are about your lifestyle, but hunting the good stuff has more to do with your outlook and approach to life than it does with your daily habits.

Hunting the good stuff essentially means focusing on the good, not the bad. The idea is that the more you intentionally notice, acknowledge, and celebrate the good things in your life, the more you'll convince yourself that your life is good indeed, making you happier and less stressed.

Hunting the good stuff doesn't necessarily mean ignoring or neglecting the bad in your life; it just means finding the good, even in the bad places.

#2: Anxiety

Anxiety is defined as a persistent feeling of worry, nervousness, or unease. It makes you feel like something bad is about to happen, but you aren't sure what or why.

Anxiety is part of everyone's life. Some have it worse than others, but we all get anxious from time to time. Sometimes, anxiety can be crippling and lead to panic attacks. That type of anxiety requires professional medical treatment and can't be managed with these tips alone. This list is intended for people with normal, day-to-day anxiety.

1. Limit Social Media Time

Study after study has shown the negative psychological effects of social media. For one, it can trigger approval anxiety. This is a feeling of inferiority when comparing yourself to others. It occurs because people on social media are usually only putting their best foot forward. Few people post about the lows of their life and only the highs. This can lead us to believe our lives aren't as good as others. This is because of "survivor's bias." Survivor bias is our tendency to believe whatever it is we see or hear without accounting for what we don't see and hear.

Social media can also trigger fear of missing out (FOMO). Seeing the highlight reel of others makes us feel like everyone around us is living life to the fullest while we're stuck in an office job. But again, what you don't see is more important than what they put out into the world. For most people, what you don't see are the same struggles you're dealing with.

2. Cut Back on Caffeine

How could anyone ever survive college without coffee? Well, no worries. You don't have to quit coffee entirely, but you definitely want to avoid *over-caffeination*. Over-caffeination can cause symptoms that feel like anxiety. Caffeine doesn't cause clinical anxiety, but it can make your anxiety symptoms worse. In fact, research has shown that caffeine raises the risk of having a panic attack in people who suffer from panic disorder.

3. Identify Triggers

Anxiety can be initiated by our environment. Sometimes, our triggers are tied to traumatic events, such as a car wreck. If you were T-boned in an intersection once, perhaps you wince every time you go through a light. That wince is your anxiety showing through, and the trigger is the intersection.

Learning your anxiety triggers is the first step to avoiding them.

4. Walk Away

If you've accidentally fallen into one of your triggers and your anxiety is now activated, you can always turn around and walk away. While this won't instantly cure your anxiety, it will take away the source and prevent any further escalation.

Scriptures to Overcome Anxiety:

> *Be anxious for nothing, but in everything by prayer and supplication, with thanksgiving, let your requests be made known to God; and the peace of God, which surpasses all understanding, will guard your hearts and minds through Christ Jesus.*

- Philippians 4:6-7

For I know the thoughts that I think toward you, says the Lord, thoughts of peace and not of evil, to give you a future and a hope.

- Jeremiah 29:11

Peace is what I leave with you; it is my own peace that I give you. I do not give it as the world does. Do not be worried and upset; do not be afraid.

- John 14:27

#3 Depression

The American Psychiatric Association defines depression as a medical illness negatively affecting the way we think, feel, and act. It's incredibly common, especially in the United States.

Depression zaps you of your hope, will, and motivation to do even the smallest tasks. It can lower your energy levels, change your appetite causing you to gain or lose weight, make it difficult to fall and stay asleep, or in the worst-case scenario, lead to thoughts of self-harm.

Depression is nothing to mess with. That's why you need to be prepared to catch it and treat it before it takes hold. Here are some ways to help you avoid or manage depression:

1. Challenge Your Thinking

Are your negative thoughts based in reality, or are you reading into things too much and making assumptions rather than basing them on facts? Sometimes, taking a step back and asking yourself, *"Do I know this for a fact?"* can help slow those racing negative thoughts.

2. Have a Routine

When people fall into a depression, they tend to lose motivation to do the little things. Their house gets dirty, their hygiene starts lacking, and they fall out of a good sleep routine. This can lead to a spiral as your dirty house and body make you feel even worse about yourself, and your lack of sleep drains you of any energy you may have started with.

Sticking to a solid routine can keep you up on the little daily things. Getting plenty of sleep and staying well-groomed may not cure your depression, but they'll make it easier to fight it.

3. Stay Connected

Isolation only feeds depression. You need people around you who can keep you grounded and pull you out of a spiral. Their fresh perspective might be just what you need to invalidate a negative thought. Depression naturally makes us want to feel like being alone, so it's especially important to stay vigilant against the urge to self-isolate.

Staying connected could also mean talking to a therapist. Having a therapist to talk to could make you feel heard, appreciated, and valued. Therapists are usually great listeners and can offer professional advice for recovering from depression. In some cases, they can prescribe medication to treat depression if they feel it's necessary.

4. Don't Abuse Alcohol

You might think I'm saying this just so you're scared to party hard in college. While I don't suggest partying hard in college, I promise I'm not just saying this to frighten you. There are plenty of other reasons to avoid drinking too much. The link between alcohol and depression is just one of them.

Alcohol and depression have what's called a bidirectional link. This means alcohol abuse can cause depression, and depression can cause alcohol abuse. In the same way, alcohol can magnify your depression symptoms, and depression can magnify your alcohol addiction. Now, this doesn't mean you'll develop major depressive disorder if you have a few beers on the weekend. The alcohol-depression dynamic mostly applies to those who already suffer from or are at higher risk of either depression or alcohol abuse.

5. Contact a Professional:

Sometimes exercising self-care isn't enough to keep unwanted feelings at bay. Don't be afraid to ask for help!

Most universities have medical professionals on staff that solely serve the student body. Sometimes, these services are free or come at a small cost. You can also use services like Better Help. This is an entirely virtual service, and they connect you with therapists based on a detailed questionnaire upon intake.

For individuals with chronic or unmanageable depression symptoms, physicians may prescribe antidepressants such as SSRIs (Selective Serotonin Reuptake Inhibitors) to promote better sleeping, eating, and social behavior.

SSRIs typically come with little to no side effects, but can occasionally worsen depression symptoms or trigger mania in patients with undiagnosed mental conditions such as Bipolar Disorder. If you feel your situation is complex, it may be best to schedule an appointment with a psychiatrist who can assess the full scope of your mental health.

Scriptures to Confront Depression:

The righteous cry out, and the LORD hears them; he delivers them from all their troubles.

- Psalm 34:17

Why, my soul, are you downcast? Why so disturbed within me? Put your hope in God, for I will yet praise him, my Savior and my God.

- Psalm 42:11

Praise be to the God and Father of our Lord Jesus Christ, the Father of compassion and the God of all comfort, who comforts us in all our troubles, so that we can comfort those in any trouble with the comfort we ourselves receive from God.

- 2 Corinthians 1: 3-4

I waited patiently for the LORD; he turned to me and heard my cry. He lifted me out of the slimy pit, out of the mud and mire; he set my feet on a rock and gave me a firm place to stand. He put a new song in my mouth, a hymn of praise to our God. Many will see and fear the LORD and put their trust in him.

- Psalm 40: 1-3

#4 Self-Esteem

High self-esteem is one of the most valuable things you can possess psychologically. It is highly correlated with general life satisfaction, achievement, and good relationships.

Low self-esteem is correlated with the opposite. Low self-esteem can lead to depression and anxiety, cause you to avoid challenges, and overall make it much more difficult to form relationships with others.

But there is a third type of self-esteem, which can be described as arrogance or, in severe cases, narcissism. Arrogance and narcissism are the exact opposite of self-esteem. The "esteem" in self-esteem can also mean self-respect. If you have high self-esteem, you have a high level of respect for yourself. Arrogant or narcissistic people have no respect for themselves or others. Both are marked by an intense fear of being wrong. They don't see themselves as inherently valuable and feel if they aren't right 100% of the time, they're less valuable as a person. They only consider their abilities, status, and power and are willing to run over everyone else to secure them.

Do you have **healthy self-esteem**? Here are a few questions that will help you tell:
- Are you afraid of feedback?
- Are you able to set boundaries with other people?
- Do you fear failure?
- Are you a people-pleaser?

If you answered no to all or most of those questions, you probably have a healthy level of self-esteem.

Do you have **low self-esteem?** Here are some questions that will help you tell:
- Do you avoid or dread social situations?
- Do you focus on the negatives about yourself and ignore the positives?
- Do you have trouble accepting compliments?
- Are you afraid to try new things?

If you answered yes to all or most of those questions, then you might have low self-esteem.

Narcissism, or narcissistic personality disorder, is a clinical condition requiring a professional diagnosis. This book won't offer any tips on identifying or managing narcissism as it's more appropriate to talk with your doctor about, but what we can talk about here is arrogance.

Are you an arrogant person? Here are some questions that will help you tell:
- Do you frequently interrupt others when they're talking?
- Do you have trouble masking your disinterest or boredom?
- Do you exaggerate your achievements and play down your failures?
- Do you find pleasure in getting revenge?

If you answered yes to most or all of these questions, you might be a bit arrogant.

What if you do have low self-esteem? How can you build yours up and get to a place where you accept yourself for who you are, stop people-pleasing, embrace life, and generally have better, healthier relationships? The list below is a great way to start.

1. Know Who Made You

Faith can play a big role in self-esteem. See, God knew what he was doing when he made you. He fashioned your abilities, your inabilities, your character, and your character flaws for a specific Kingdom purpose. The catch is that you might not know now (or ever) what your purpose is. It can sometimes go unseen, but that doesn't mean you don't have one. Trust that God is using you whether you know it or not.

As Christians, we believe that every creature, man, and animal is unconditionally and eternally loved by our creator. That means you too! If you allow this realization to shape your sense of self-worth, nobody will ever be able to take it from you.

2. Focus on Your Strengths

Even if they don't show it, every person you've ever met has felt like a failure at some point. But failing at something doesn't make *you* a failure; it just means you're talented at other things. We can't all be good at everything. It's impossible! Thankfully, there are people who are fantastic at the things we're terrible at. This is how the world goes round.

The Apostle Paul describes this idea as the "body of Christ."

Yes, the body has many different parts, not just one part. If the foot says, "I am not a part of the body because I am not a hand," that does not make it any less a part of the body. And if the ear says, "I am not part of the body because I am not an eye," would that make it any less a part of the body? If the whole body were an eye, how would you hear? Or if your whole body were an ear, how would you smell anything?

• 1 Corinthians 12:14-17

What a way to sum it up! The foot is not inferior to the hand because it can't turn a doorknob, and the hand is not inferior to the foot because it can't support the body's weight. They each serve their own role. So it is with our place in the Lord's kingdom.

3. Start Saying No

Learning to say no, even when the other person won't be happy to hear it, is a great way to practice establishing boundaries. Boundaries are the rules or limits we set for ourselves in a relationship. They're how we keep from being taken advantage of, abused, or overburdened. People with low self-esteem tend to have a hard time saying no. This is because they value the other person's feelings more than their own preferences due to their distorted sense of self-worth. This is a recipe for disaster in any relationship and may lead to deep resentment and anger.

As you get older, you'll learn that you're not responsible for other people's feelings as long as you have acted in a Christ-like way. If someone gets angry with you because you told them no and refused to go against one of your values, then so be it. You don't owe them your integrity, and it's okay to put your foot down. One thing I wish I realized at a younger age is that it's entirely possible to be assertive and polite at the same time.

4. Give Yourself Goals

The key here is choosing goals you can actually accomplish so you can feel good about yourself when you do. This builds self-esteem bit by bit, so setting goals that are too lofty defeats the purpose.

When setting goals for yourself, first sit down and figure out what your end is. What is something you want to be or do? For example: *"I'm a guitar player."* If this is your end, then your goals should be made up of smaller pieces of it. Don't sit down with a guitar and say, *"I'm not getting up until I can call myself a guitar player."* How productive would that be? Not at all! In fact, it would be counterproductive because you would quickly lose hope and feel defeated like there's no end in sight.

A better strategy is to break up your goals into bite-sized chunks. To be able to call yourself a guitar player, you need to know your triads, bar chords, scales, picking techniques, and more. All of these skills you can pursue individually. Set yourself a goal to learn how to play every major chord, A through G. Tackle one chord during each practice session, and within a week, I bet you can play seven more chords than you could at the beginning of the week. When you accomplish that goal, you'll not only feel good about yourself, but you'll objectively be a better guitar player. Then, move on to the next skill.

Scriptures to Overcome Fear:

For God did not give us a spirit of fear, but of power and of love and a sound mind.

• 2 Timothy 1:7

He will never leave you nor forsake you. Do not be afraid; do not be discouraged.

• Deuteronomy 31:8

Don't fear, for I have redeemed you; I have called you by name; you are Mine.

• Isaiah 43:1

Fear not, for I am with you; Be not dismayed, for I am your God. I will strengthen you, yes, I will help you, I will uphold you with My righteous right hand.

• Isaiah 41:10

Pray this Prayer

Lord, help me to care for my mental health. Give me the strength to prioritize rest when I'm over-stressed and fight off anxiety, depression, and low self-esteem. Remind me that you made me in your image and that I have infinite worth in your eyes.

Chapter 7

Finding Your Purpose

"You can make many plans, but the Lord's purpose will prevail."
- Proverbs 19:21

In the previous chapter, I mentioned that God has a purpose for your life, whether you know it or not. Right now, it may seem like your purpose is to graduate college with decent grades. I would call that a short-term goal, not a long-term, God-given purpose.

Everyone's purpose has two parts. We all share the first part in common: becoming more like Christ. Every Christian is called to be as Christ-like as possible. Being a Christian is defined by being Christ-like. If your goal isn't to become more Christ-like, then I think there's a solid argument you aren't a Christian at all.

If God is love (1 John 4:8), then becoming more like God means becoming more loving. This is God's ultimate purpose for us, and it supersedes all others. Its importance is explained by Paul in 1 Corinthians 13:1-3:

If I could speak all the languages of earth and of angels but didn't love others, I would only be a noisy gong or a clanging cymbal. If I had the gift of prophecy, and if I understood all of God's secret plans and possessed all knowledge, and if I had such faith that I could move mountains but didn't love others, I would be nothing. If I gave everything I had to the poor and even sacrificed my body, I could boast about it, but if I didn't love others, I would have gained nothing.

Paul goes on to define love in verses 4-7:

Love is patient and kind. Love is not jealous or boastful or proud or rude. It does not demand its own way. It is not irritable, and it keeps no record of being wronged. It does not rejoice about injustice but rejoices whenever the truth wins out. Love never gives up, never loses faith, is always hopeful, and endures through every circumstance.

Until we become these things, the second part of our purpose doesn't matter. Until we love like Christ, all else is just a waste of time.

What is My Second Purpose?

Your second purpose can be a bit elusive. It can also be called your *"calling."* Many people refer to a purpose as a calling because it was their experience that God "called" out to them and told them.

It takes many people years to hear a clear calling from God. For whatever reason, God doesn't always tell us outright what He wants us to do or focus on. Instead, He gives us subtle hints and whispers of guidance. While this is really annoying, most people will tell you it's not about the destination but the journey, and that what you learn on the journey of discovering your purpose is well worth the wait.

There are a few things that can help you discover your second purpose. They're listed below. The idea is that your second purpose is a combination of all 4. Doing just one will only get you so far. You need to do them all to get the clearest picture of your second purpose as possible. Once you do all 4 of these things, sit down and see if there is any overlap. If one thing pops up in 2 or 3 of the things below, that could be a tip that you're getting warmer.

#1: Know Your Spiritual Gifts

Spiritual gifts, or *"gifts of the Holy Spirit,"* are how God expresses his power through us. They're abilities specifically given to us to help grow the Church. Spiritual gifts are not the same as talents. Talents can be worked at, developed, and improved. But spiritual gifts? Those you either have or you don't. They're given to us and, therefore, aren't a product of anything we can do.

Everyone has the potential to unlock a spiritual gift. When you become a Christian and receive the Holy Spirit, you're eligible for a spiritual gift. But of course, this logically means there are a lot of people out there walking around without a spiritual gift. If you don't know what your spiritual gift is, that means you either don't have one or just haven't discovered what it is yet.

There are a handful of spiritual gifts. The Bible discusses them sparingly, and most of what is said is written by Paul. There isn't one official list of spiritual gifts. There isn't a single verse containing all spiritual gifts.

Rather, the lists of spiritual gifts you can find on the internet and in books are a collection of some verses addressing spiritual gifts. One example is 1 Corinthians 12:7-11:

A spiritual gift is given to each of us so we can help each other. To one person, the Spirit gives the ability to give wise advice; to another, the same Spirit gives a message of special knowledge. The same Spirit gives great faith to another, and to someone else the Spirit gives the gift of healing. He gives one person the power to perform miracles, and another the ability to prophesy. He gives someone else the ability to discern whether a message is from the Spirit of God or from another spirit. Still another person is given the ability to speak in unknown languages, while another is given the ability to interpret what is being said. It is the one and only Spirit who distributes all these gifts. He alone decides which gift each person should have.

From this passage and others, Biblical scholars have distilled conventionally accepted spiritual gifts. Here's a list of spiritual gifts along with their definitions according to Tyndale House Publishing:

1. **Administration**: The ability to help steer the church, or a ministry, toward the successful completion of God-given goals with skills in planning, organization, and supervision.
2. **Missions**: A person sent to new places with the Gospel.
3. **Discernment**: The wisdom to recognize truth from untruth by correctly evaluating whether a behavior or teaching is from God or another ungodly source.
4. **Evangelism**: The ability to successfully communicate the message of the Gospel, especially to nonbelievers.

5. **Exhortation**: Competence in offering encouragement, comfort, and support to help someone be all God wants them to be.
6. **Faith**: People with this gift have such great confidence in the power and promises of God that they can stand strong in their belief, no matter what may try to shake them. They can also stand up for the church and for their faith in such a way as to defend and move it forward.
7. **Giving**: Those who have this gift are particularly willing and able to share what resources they have with pleasure and without the need to see them returned.
8. **Healing**: A capability used by God to restore others, be that physically, emotionally, mentally, or spiritually.

9. **Helps**: Someone with this gift is able to support or assist members of the body of Christ so that they may be free to minister to others.
10. **Hospitality**: A natural ability to make people—even strangers—feel welcome in one's own home or church as a means to disciple or serve them.
11. **Knowledge**: This is the gift of someone who actively pursues knowledge of the Bible. This person may also enjoy analyzing biblical data.
12. **Leadership**: This aptitude marks a person who is able to stand before a church, direct the body with care and attention, and motivate them toward achieving the church's goals.
13. **Mercy**: This is the defining trait of a person with great sensitivity for those who are suffering. It manifests itself in offering compassion, encouragement, and love for giving practical help to someone in need.
14. **Prophecy**: The ability to speak the message of God to others. This

sometimes involves foresight or visions of what is to come. This skill should be used only to offer encouragement or warning.

15. **Serving**: A talent for identifying tasks needed for the body of Christ and using available resources to get the job done.
16. **Teaching/shepherding**: The skill to teach from the Bible and communicate it effectively for the understanding and spiritual growth of others.
17. **Wisdom**: The gift of being able to sort through facts and data to discover what needs to be done for the church.

How to Find Your Spiritual Gifts

How do you know which of the gifts listed above you have? Well, thanks to the wonderful day and age we live in, you can just take a test! I suggest this one created by Cru, the Christian campus organization mentioned earlier:

https://www.cru.org/us/en/train-and-grow/quizzes-and-assessments/what-type-of-spiritual-gifts-do-you-have-quiz

You can also ask your friends and family. They may see something in you that you don't and be able to offer a fresh perspective as to what your gifts are. Another possibility is a class offered by your church. Some churches offer Sunday school or online classes that help you determine your spiritual gifts.

#2 Find Your Passion

What do you like to do? What hobbies interest you? Is there something in your life that grabs your attention and doesn't let go? If so, that thing could very well be your passion. A passion piques your excitement or interest and brings you feelings of satisfaction and contribution. A passion is also usually something you're naturally good at.

It's easy to get passion and purpose confused. It's essential to remember that while they're closely related, they're different. Your purpose is related to your passion in that your passion enables your purpose. Passion keeps us motivated and pointed toward our purpose. If purpose is the road, passion is the gas in your car.

A passion doesn't have to be a job or an activity; it can be a feeling or cause. Some people are passionate about helping others. They're probably well suited in non-profit and volunteer work. If you like solving problems, you might be interested in coding or engineering.

If you don't know what you're passionate about yet, that's okay! You're still young and have plenty of time. College will help you a lot in uncovering the things that get you out of bed in the morning.

How to Find Your Passion:

These three questions will also help you determine where your passions lie. I highly recommend sitting down and putting a lot of thought into your answers. Write them down, then set a reminder in your phone for 6 months. After the 6 months are up, re-answer the questions and compare your answers now with your answers 6 months ago. If they're both the same, that could be a huge hint toward a lasting passion.

1. What do you love to talk and learn about?

Ever met someone who was just a total nerd about a certain topic? Maybe it was video games, WWII history, or *The Lord of the Rings*. They could name every single random fact about that thing. When these people aren't talking about their obsession, they're learning about it. When they aren't learning about their obsession, they're talking about it. They always have it on their mind. I'm exaggerating a little bit, of course. It's not possible to think about one thing 100% of the time. But do you have one train of thought standing out among the rest?

Is there a certain subject that always seems to pop in your head? Your mind could ponder a million other things. Why this particular thing? It's because that thing is likely closely related to your passion.

2. Are you inclined toward people, places, systems, creativity, or animals?

An inclination is a preference or tendency that comes naturally to us for no apparent reason. They're feelings we're born with. An inclination toward people means you like assisting, interacting with, working with, or working around people. An inclination toward places means you like to travel, see and try new things, and generally be unburdened by possessions. Having nothing but what's in your suitcase may sound stressful and risky, but it can also be surprisingly liberating. If you have an inclination toward systems, you like when things take inputs and create outputs that connect end to end with multiple steps in between.

If you're creatively inclined, you probably like making things from scratch. Whether it's music, painting, writing, or drawing, creating something always starts with a blank slate and will only ever become what you make of it.

Think about these categories and what jobs might satisfy each one, or in some cases, more than one. Once you identify a few careers that fit your inclinations, you can start doing research to determine whether you'd actually like them or not in the long-term.

For example, if you love places, you might enjoy a career as a pilot. Few people travel to new places as often as pilots. You also might like to be a traveling salesman. A life in that profession can involve traveling to a new city multiple times a week.

If you like systems, then the worlds of computer engineering, mechanics, philosophy, math, or other technical fields could be for you. If you love animals, then a career as a veterinarian could be yours.

Your passion can be a mix of these categories as well. There are plenty of jobs out there that hit on multiple. Take sales as an example again. If you like traveling, then you probably like people too. When you travel, you're constantly around people and often make new connections. So being a traveling salesman would not only take you to new places, but it'll give you plenty of time around people.

3. What would you be willing to do for free?
Show me where you spend your time, and I'll show you your passion. Time is our most important resource. It's valuable because it's so limited and constantly running out. We never have enough time. You might say

money is our most important resource, but you can't have money without time. Money is just a representation of our labor, which requires time or skills built by time in school or the workforce. So, time is certainly our most valuable asset.

If you're willing to use your most important resource for nothing in return, then whatever you're using it on is extremely important to you and is likely closely related to your passion. Most of us have activities in our lives like this. Many pilots would tell you they would fly for free if they didn't have so many bills. They just love to fly that much. Many artists spend years honing their craft and creating for nothing in return. They simply hope someday, their efforts will be rewarded.

#3 Ask a Mentor

A mentor is fundamentally a counselor. They're someone you can learn from and whose footsteps you can follow in. They offer advice, guidance, and support for different aspects of your life. Depending on what area you're looking for help with, a mentor can counsel you on your career, marriage, education, or parenting. The Bible is very pro-mentor:

Keep putting into practice all you learned and received from me—everything you heard from me and saw me doing. Then, the God of peace will be with you.
• Philippians 4:9

Remember your leaders who taught you the Word of God. Think of all the good that has come from their lives, and follow the example of their faith.
• Hebrews 13:7

But you must remain faithful to the things you have been taught. You know they are true, for you know you can trust those who taught you.

• 2 Timothy 3:14

One of the most prominent personal relationships depicted in the Bible by Paul and Timothy was mentorship. Paul wrote to Timothy on two occasions (1 and 2 Timothy) encouraging, teaching, and correcting him. Because of Paul's guidance and the power of the Holy Spirit, Timothy was able to build a successful branch of the new church in Ephesus. What was Jesus to the 12 Disciples if not a mentor (aside from being the Messiah)?

Fundamentally, a mentor should be someone who is or has been where you want to be. That's why they're so valuable, as they can offer you insider information into how to accomplish your goals and become the sort of person you want to be. Mentors usually offer advice based on their own experience or from what they've observed in others over the course of their careers.

For a mentor to be able to advise you in finding your purpose, they need to get to know you as a person. Because your purpose is so closely related to who you are and your God-given abilities, a mentor could never properly steer you in the right direction if they didn't first build a relationship with you. So, be prepared to spend a significant amount of time with your mentor.

Because a mentor knows who you are, they know your spiritual gifts, passions, and inclinations and can spot them better than you sometimes. They're able to cross-reference their experience with your passion and abilities and give you recommendations for what they think would lead to a fulfilling life. Mentors can save you a lot of time and heartache. There are 1,000 ways to do something wrong, but usually one way to do it right. Why waste time and energy blazing your own trail when a mentor can show you the easiest, fastest path?

How to Find a Mentor

Start by asking your family. Once you choose your major, ask around and see if you have any family who has worked in that field. Once you decide what your passion is, ask if any of them have the same one or if they've successfully built a life that satisfies their passion. You can also ask them if they have any friends or acquaintances who have done the same.

If asking family doesn't work out, you have many other great options available now that you're entering college. Many people find college mentors through their degree programs or other collegiate activities they're involved in. Once you choose a major, your mentor could potentially be a professor, your academic advisor, a teaching assistant, or someone you worked for during an internship. If you get involved in an on-campus ministry such as Cru or Navigators, your mentor could be someone you met through those groups.

Put yourself in the same places as people you want to be like, and you'll have a good shot at landing a mentor who helps you crush your goals. The trick is to always be on the lookout and not be afraid to talk to them. It takes guts to approach an older, accomplished adult and ask for their time. A good mentor will recognize that, and it will likely improve your odds of getting a "yes".

Once you find someone you think would make a good mentor, you want to have a formal conversation where you ask if they'll be your mentor. Setting up a mentorship should be a deliberate act. You should literally set a meeting with them, then ask point-blank, *"Would you be interested in being my mentor?"* Mentorships can happen naturally, but it's best to be forthright with why you want to build a relationship with that person. It's possible they could feel taken advantage of if they find out you've been spending time with them just to get your hands on their knowledge and connections.

#4 Pray About It

Be sure to pray about numbers 1-3 above. What better way to find your God-given purpose than to ask the Big Man himself? These are concrete things you can include in your routine prayers:

"God, guide me on my journey to discovering my spiritual gifts and passions."

"God, connect me with a mentor."

Another concrete thing you can pray for when asking God for your purpose is **wisdom.** Wisdom is your capacity to see things from God's perspective. Wisdom changes the way you think. Paul talks about this in Romans 12:2:

Don't copy the behavior and customs of this world, but let God transform you into a new person by changing the way you think. Then you will learn to know God's will for you, which is good and pleasing and perfect.

Wisdom helps us to make good decisions and to put the right "spin" on life. When things go wrong or you're suffering, wisdom helps you to understand why. If you can't understand why, wisdom helps you walk in faith and trust that God has a reason. It helps you give God the benefit of the doubt that it's all part of the plan. Without wisdom, problems and suffering make you angry. With wisdom, problems and suffering teach you lessons.

A lot can be accomplished through consistent, honest, heartfelt prayer, but you have to be willing to be patient. God has his own timeline, and when you've been around for eternity, a few years is like a blink of an eye.

> **Pray this Prayer**
> *Lord, show me my purpose. I want to know what it is so I can pursue it in obedience. Grant me the wisdom to catch your signs and hints and pursue the passions that matter. Send me a mentor who can advise and counsel me on my path in life. Lord, speak to me and tell me my spiritual gifts.*

Chapter 8

Keeping the Faith

"I have fought the good fight, I have finished the race, and I have remained faithful."
- 2 Timothy 4:7

Let's bring things full circle. In the introduction to this book, I said that with college comes independence. Once you start college, for the first time in your life, you won't be under the thumb of your parents. They won't dictate your schedule; you will. They won't provide you with meals, you will. They won't do your laundry. *You will!*

Not only are you no longer under the thumb of your parents, but you're no longer under the thumb of an overbearing education system. Gone are the days when you must raise your hand to use the restroom. Gone are the days when you even have to show up at all!

College professors are not like your high school teachers. They don't care if you pass or fail their class. Many revel in having a high fail rate! They won't call your parents if you don't show up to school or give you a detention for being on your phone in class. As long as you're not disrupting others, professors likely don't care if you're even conscious during their class. It's now on you to make sure what needs doing gets done.

This goes for your faith as well. No one is going to drag you to church on Sunday mornings. No one is going to make you do a daily devotional or maintain your prayer life. Your faith is now your own. Will you go all in or not? It's up to you. The only thing you can't be is lukewarm.

> *But since you are like lukewarm water, neither hot nor cold, I will spit you out of my mouth!*
>
> • Revelation 3:16

Trust me, keeping the faith in college is not easy. The distractions, temptations, and counter-arguments to your beliefs will be endless. That's why you need to prepare.

Unfortunately, there is a growing number of kids just like you who lose their faith in college. The stats are pretty startling. Several studies have found that nearly 66% of teenagers who profess Christianity before college lose their faith during college. That's millions of people! What can you call it besides an epidemic?

Some common reasons for this are just that, changes in life situations like moving to college, disagreeing with the church's stance on political or social issues, and work responsibilities.
Many will just no longer attend church. Another reason, some feel members seem judgmental or hypocritical and no longer feel connected

to people in their church.

I hope and pray this doesn't happen to you. I hope you're able to keep the faith during this formative time of your life. Here are a few things to help you do so.

How to Keep the Faith

The counter-arguments to your Christian beliefs will be endless in college. There are a lot of atheists in academia, and they're all really smart. If you engage with an atheist professor on the matter of religion and go in unprepared, you could risk having your entire world turned upside down.

What ends up happening to a lot of young Christians in college is they're presented with information about the Bible they haven't seen before. This information is usually in support of the idea that the Bible is a load of crap, or simply isn't from God. They'll have compelling arguments against the existence of God as well.

1. Study Apologetics

How do you process interactions with people who challenge your Christian beliefs without altogether losing your faith? You study apologetics.

Apologetics is "the intellectual defense of the truth of the Christian religion." Apologetics is how many people build the foundations of their faith. Not everyone has had spiritual or unexplainable experiences that lead them to a belief in God. These people need evidence and arguments in order to come to faith. Apologetics provides evidence and arguments.

Here are a few great books on apologetics I highly recommend reading:
- **Letters from a Skeptic**, by Greg Boyd
- **Mere Christianity**, by C.S. Lewis
- **A Shot of Faith (to the Head)**, by Mitch Stokes
- **The Case for Christ**, by Lee Strobel
- **The Reason for God**, by Timothy Keller
- **Jesus the Christ**, by James E. Talmage

All of these books address common questions and arguments atheists, skeptics, and even believers have about Christianity.

Reading these books won't make you an expert at apologetics. It won't make you any more equipped to "debunk" an atheist professor if you encounter one (they're just too smart and have read more than you). But what reading them will do is expose you to good arguments in favor of Christianity. They'll show you that even though atheists and skeptics have good points and strong arguments for their beliefs, smart people have thought of good, strong rebuttals. Reading these books will strengthen your faith and keep you from being shaken too hard by the opposition.

2. Don't Be Afraid to Doubt

Doubt leads to questions. Questions lead to a search for answers. Few people spend more time investigating their faith than those with doubts. In a sense, doubt leads to education.

The Bible doesn't forbid doubt. What it does is offer encouragement for those who doubt and instructions for helping others who are doubting:

Then Jesus told them, "I tell you the truth, if you have faith and don't doubt, you can do things like this and much more. You can even say to this mountain, 'May you be lifted up and thrown into the sea,' and it will happen."

• Matthew 21:21

And you must show mercy to those whose faith is wavering. Rescue others by snatching them from the flames of judgment. Show mercy to still others, but do so with great caution, hating the sins that contaminate their lives.

• Jude 1:22-23

Doubt is not unwise, either. Many pastors will encourage you to ask questions about God and the Bible. They understand that unresolved doubts and questions cause more harm than the doubts themselves.

One of my favorite theologians and apologists, Greg Boyd, tells the story (in his book listed above) of losing his faith almost as soon as he stepped foot on campus. At the time, he was a member of a Pentecostal church that discouraged questioning the confusing parts of the Bible. Specifically, he mentions noticing a few inconsistencies and errors in the Bible.

When he approached his pastor and asked about these errors and inconsistencies, his pastor responded by asking if Boyd was engaging in premarital sex because, in his experience, people who have doubts are sinning in other areas of their lives. Needless to say, this was a disappointing response for Boyd. A semester or two later, he took a class where the professor made a convincing argument claiming the same errors and inconsistencies Boyd had already noticed discredited the entire Bible. That was that. Shortly after, he lost his faith.

Thankfully, Boyd found his way back and is now one of the best apologists out there (in my opinion). He didn't find his way back to faith by ignoring his questions and blindly believing. He came back to faith by studying apologetics. By exposing himself to the counter-arguments and explanations for the arguments that caused him to lose his faith, he realized that the Bible is true and God is real. We also can learn from him, to doubt our doubts before our faith.

So don't be afraid or ashamed to voice your doubts and *seek* answers. Doing so will strengthen your faith as well as your intellect.

3. Build a Christian Community

Accountability is a prominent teaching in the Bible. There are verses about holding each other accountable:

Confess your sins to each other and pray for each other so that you may be healed.

- James 5:16

There are verses on God holding us all accountable:

Nothing in all creation is hidden from God. Everything is naked and exposed before his eyes, and he is the one to whom we are accountable.
- Hebrews 4:13

One of the best things about having a Christian community is that it can hold you accountable. When you're straying too far off the path, a Christian community can keep you accountable and pull you back on. If you're getting apathetic or complacent, a solid Christian community can rejuvenate and challenge you to be better.

These communities also act as a support network. Christians are called to care for their neighbors and for the least of these. If a group of Christians sees one of their members struggling, it is the group's Christian duty to help however they can. If you have a community of Christians, you become a part of that support network. That means you take when you need but also have to give when you can.

Support from a solid Christian community can make all the difference in grounding your faith.

To Wrap it up.

How does working in a way that brings glory to God, finding Christian friends, a Christian significant other, finding a church, caring for your mental health, and finding your purpose help you keep the faith?

Knowing our work should reflect our faith and bring glory to God helps us get through the times when work is boring, feels pointless, or is just really challenging. It helps you maintain a level of attention to detail that will put your assignments and exams in front of the rest of your class. Helping someone else and bringing glory to God with our talents, skills and passions make it all worth it!

Finding Christian friends helps you keep the faith by acting as an important part of your Christian community. The same goes for finding a Christian significant other and finding a church. All of these together will form your Christian community, which acts as a support network when your faith is a little shaky. They're also a great resource for the times you're doubting. A good Christian community will hear your doubts and reassure you the best they can. Odds are, someone in your community has had the same doubts at some point and can give you the explanation or counter-argument that helped them.

Keeping tabs on your mental health keeps your faith strong in the same way exercise keeps your body and immune system strong. With good mental health, you can fight off Satan's little jabs more effectively. Satan's lies are much more tempting when we're depressed or having an anxiety episode. It's tough to fight the enemy if we're not in a good place mentally.

"Put on the whole armor of God, that you may be able to stand against the wiles of the devil. For we do not wrestle against flesh and blood, but against principalities, against powers, against the rulers of darkness in this age, against spiritual hosts of wickedness in the heavenly places. Therefore, take up the whole armor of God, that you may be able to withstand in the evil day, and having done all, to stand."

- Ephesians 6:11-13

Finally, finding your purpose helps you keep the faith by pointing you in the right direction. Wandering aimlessly through life becomes tiresome after a point. It drains your motivation and your vigor. Knowing your purpose–your north star–keeps you feeling accomplished and like your life and time matter.

Absorb and implement these things, and watch what God does for you in college!

> **Pray this Prayer**
> *I pray I keep the faith in college. Help me to push through the times when homework and exams seem to be too much and to remember the outcome is for your glory. Send me Christian friends, a Christian significant other, and place me in a solid church. Help me care for my mental health and show me my purpose, Lord. I pray I can build a great Christian community. Lord, help me to know what I believe and why I believe it. In your name, Amen.*

Thank you and what's coming!

Thank you for picking up my book! I hope you've found this guide helpful and received some unique value and learned something new.

While this book covered a few of the most essential aspects of being a Christian in college, it doesn't cover everything. There's so much advice out there you could benefit from that we've barely scratched the surface. I will be writing more in the future and hope you will join my email list for the up coming books and a few emails here and there covering Christian devotionals and/or self-help.

Click below or scan the QR code for those upcoming book promotions, email's and free resources. https://lapublishings.aweb.page/p/a7e17635-be2a-486f-88f2-2c4ae99cb100

The Journal download is one you can print, or type write into for easy access wherever you go to keep thoughts during the day. This journal is your space to reflect on your faith journey, with meaningful prayer and gratitude tracking pages, and to collect your college experiences. Including pages with this book's prayers and scriptures.

I would truly appreciate your feedback!! If you found this book to be a good read, be sure to tell your friends! When you share your positive feedback in a review, and I read them all, it will help others, also to find the book. When they find it, they too can see the way Christian living in college may be just as wonderful and helpful. May God be with you and have a great time in college!   (QR Code for Reviewing on Amazon!)

References

Chapter 1 - https://www.princetonreview.com/quiz/career-quiz

Chapter 2 - Books available - Barclay's Daily Study Bible - Bible Commentaries. StudyLight.org. (n.d.). https://www.studylight.org/commentaries/eng/dsb/matthew-25.html. and Mueller, P. A., Oppenheimer, D.M. "The Pen Is Mightier Than the Keyboard: Advantages of Longhand Over Laptop Note Taking." Psychological Science 25, no. 6 (2014): 1159–1168. https://doi.org/10.1177/0956797614524581.

Physiological science article, the bbe:

Roessingh, H., U. of C. (2022, February 28). The Benefits of Note-Taking by Hand. BBC Worklife. https://www.bbc.com/worklife/article/20200910-the-benefits-of-note-taking-by-hand

Effective note-taking.

University of North Carolina. (2023, September 12). "Effective Note-Taking in Class." UNC Learning Center.

Mimic the exam conditions.

Does Listening to Music Really Help You Study? – The College of Arts & Sciences at Texas A&M University. (2021, March 10). https://liberalarts.tamu.edu/blog/2021/03/10/does-listening-to-music-really-help-you-study/

Silence your phone and put it in your bag or....

Alcaraz, M. L., Labonté-LeMoyne, É., Lupien, S., Sénécal, S., Cameron, A.-F., Bellavance, F., & Léger, P.-M. (2022). Stress Can Lead to an Increase in Smartphone Use in the Context of Texting While Walking. Frontiers in Psychology, 13. https://doi.org/10.3389/fpsyg.2022.760107

Adjust your environment

Mechanical and Biomedical Engineering, & Larson, J. (2021, April 20). 5 Ways to Stop Procrastinating. Mechanical and Biomedical Engineering. https://www.boisestate.edu/coen-mbe/2021/04/20/5-ways-to-stop-procrastinating/

Keep tasks achievable

Clear, J. (2022, August 31) Procrastination: A Scientific Guide on How to Stop Procrastinating. James Clear.

https://jamesclear.com/procrastination

Chapter 3 - Church is people, not a place.

Staff, B. A. S. (2022, October 13). The House of Peter: The Home of Jesus in Capernaum? https://www.biblicalarchaeology.org/daily/biblical-sites-places/biblical-archaeology-sites/the-house-of-peter-the-home-of-jesus-in-capernaum/

Clarke says that the author.......a friend sharpens a friend

Clarke, A. (n.d.). "Commentary on Proverbs 27." The Adam Clarke Commentary.

https://www.studylight.org/commentaries/eng/acc/proverbs-27.html

Chapter 5 - The consensus is that there is no such thing as a normal sex drive....

MediLexicon International. (n.d.). Mismatched Sex Drives: Relationships and Coping. Medical News Today.

https://www.medicalnewstoday.com/articles/mismatched-sex-drives#summary

In, fact according to Psychology today, frequency is the number one sex related argument between married couples.

Sussex Publishers. (2018). How to Agree on Sexual Frequency. Psychology Today.

https://www.psychologytoday.com/us/blog/married-and-still-doing-it/201806/how-agree-sexual-frequency

Chapter 6 - The term mental health was never used by the medical community until 1946

Bertolote, J. The Roots of the Concept of Mental Health. World Psychiatry. 2008;7(2):113-6. doi: 10.1002/j.2051-5545.2008.tb00172.x. PMID: 18560478; PMCID: PMC2408392.

Change you body, change your mind

Brian Hesler, M. D. (2023, February 21). Five Tips to Manage Your Stress. Mayo Clinic Health System.

https://www.mayoclinichealthsystem.org/hometown-health/speaking-of-health/5-tips-to-manage-stress

Take time to decompress.

doing so can help build synapse pathways and form, clearer memories.

Sandoiu, A. MediLexicon International. (2018, May 6). Quiet Rest After Learning Helps us to Remember the Fine Details. Medical News Today.

https://www.medicalnewstoday.com/articles/321723

Limit social media time

Wolfers, L. N. (2022a, January 31). Social media use, stress, and coping. Current Opinion in Psychology.

https://www.sciencedirect.com/science/article/pii/S2352250X22000070

Cut back on caffeine.

in fact, research has shown that caffeine raises the risk of having a panic attack..

Klevebrant, L., & Frick, A. (2022). Effects of Caffeine on Anxiety and Panic Attacks in Patients with Panic Disorder: A Systematic Review and Meta-Analysis. General Hospital Psychiatry, 74, 22–31.

https://doi.org/10.1016/j.genhosppsych.2021.11.005

The alcohol-depression dynamic mostly applies to those who already suffer from or are at high risk of either depression or alcohol abuse.

Mosel, Stacy M.S.W., (2023, June 9). Alcohol and Depression: The Link Between Alcoholism and Depression. American Addiction Centers.

https://americanaddictioncenters.org/alcoholism-treatment/depression

Self- Esteem

Sussex Publishers. (n.d.-b). Self-Esteem. Psychology Today.

https://www.psychologytoday.com/us/basics/self-esteem

Chapter 7 - above administration

Unfolding Faith. Unfolding Faith Blog. (2019, October 1).

https://www.tyndale.com/sites/unfoldingfaithblog/2019/10/01/a-quick-list-of-biblical-spiritual-gifts-which-gifts-exist-and-what-they-mean

Chapter 8 - Christianity before college lose their faith during college

Earls, A. (2023a, June 8). Most Teenagers Drop Out of Church When They Become Young Adults. Lifeway Research. https://research.lifeway.com/2019/01/15/most-teenagers-drop-out-of-church-as-young-adults/

Study apologetics

Grace Theological Seminary. (2023, October 11). What is Apologetics? https://seminary.grace.edu/what-is-apologetics/

About Peter Christian

Peter Christian is a passionate writer who specializes in the self-development space. His writing is a credit to his enthusiasm to providing guidance for young adults and adults to look inward and focus on ways to better oneself.

Peter's love for writing began early on and during his college years when he met his wife is when he was encouraged to really write things down. Together they have built a beautiful family, who inspires much of his work. He grew up surrounded by lots of family members and community that shaped his understanding of relationships, parenting, and the importance of self-development.

His active involvement in church youth ministry has given him valuable insights into the challenges faced by today's youth. Peter has encountered many children and teens dealing with depression and anxiety. This experience fuels his passion for researching techniques and ideas to better serve these students.

Peter also provides guidance to parents on how to understand their children better and themselves better. He doesn't claim to know everything, he offers his experience and thorough research. His advice is rooted in how self-improvement is the key to having changes in your life and your home. Peters' values, principles and developed skills have guided him throughout his life, and he wants to share that in the written word with you.

In addition to writing, Peter enjoys being with his family, music, reading and spending time outdoors as places that bring him happiness. He also actively contributes to his community through various initiatives.

Readers of Peter's words often express appreciation for the practical advice he offers based on real-life experiences. If you're seeking guidance on navigating adulthood, parenting, or a life coach from someone that has been there, Peter Christian's books are an excellent resource.

Made in United States
North Haven, CT
03 June 2024